BLACK
ODYSSEY

BLACK ODYSSEY

The Afro-American Ordeal in Slavery

BY

Nathan Irvin Huggins

VINTAGE BOOKS
A Division of Random House
New York

VINTAGE BOOKS EDITION, January 1979

Copyright © 1977 by Nathan Irvin Huggins

Library of Congress Cataloging in Publication Data

Huggins, Nathan Irvin, 1927–
  Black odyssey.

  Bibliography: p.
  1. Slavery in the United States—History.
2. Slavery in the United States—Condition of slaves.
I. Title.
[E441.H89 1979]   301.44'93'0973   78-4793
ISBN 0–394–72687–1

Printed in Canada

Contents

Acknowledgments

I WOULD LIKE to thank a number of people and some institutions for helping make this book possible.

A Guggenheim fellowship supported research during my sabbatical year. The Ford Foundation gave me money to travel and talk with people in several African countries.

I used many libraries in this country, and I am especially grateful to John Price and his staff at Louisiana State University Archives at Baton Rouge and to Isaac Copeland and Carolyn Wallace of the Southern Collection at North Carolina University at Chapel Hill.

Many West African scholars were generous with their time and knowledge: SENEGAL: Chiek Anta Diop and M'Baye Guéye at Dakar; GHANA: Adu Bohene of Legon; NIGERIA: J. F. Ade Ajayi (presently at Lagos), O. Ikime, O. Onoge, E. B. Idowa, and E. U. Essien-Udom, of Ibadan; and Robin Horton of Ifé University.

My most profound education in Africa came, however, from a too brief emersion in village life. For that priceless experience I am forever obliged to Emanuel

Nsiah of Accra, Ghana, and especially to Henry Amoo Adjei—herbalist, "doctor," mystic, teacher, guide, and "linguister"—who translated me into a world I would otherwise never have known.

Two early teachers have influenced me in many ways, but certainly in this book. Kenneth Stampp insisted, long before others, that slaves had something to tell us about slavery. Oscar Handlin showed me, by example, that scholarship was compatible with personal vision. Although I know that each will find something in this book to criticize, I hope they will discover in it the genuine respect I feel for them.

I benefited from comments and suggestions of Herbert Gutman and Herbert Klein, who took time from busy schedules to read the manuscript. I am especially grateful to Peter Wood for his careful and detailed commentary. I hope that these friends will see where their efforts have improved the book and will not mind where I have not accepted their suggestions.

I would like to thank Ms. Valencia Ortiz for typing the manuscript under considerable pressure.

This book owes much to my editors, Thomas Engelhardt and Donna Grusky Bass, who cared for it and, therefore, made our work enjoyable.

I have dedicated this book to my wife, Brenda Carlita Huggins, who contributed to it at every stage. She gave of her time to follow me into Southern archives. She brought her special insight to the understanding of African priestesses and village life. Most important, she encouraged me when my spirits flagged, never allowing me to forget to trust my own vision.

Introduction

MOST AMERICANS think slavery was a strange and ironic fact in a national history characterized by personal liberty and liberal democracy. The slave's story, therefore, would be one of a valiant if vain struggle to be accepted as part of that mainstream. I have come to think, however, that in making racial slavery crucial to its social and economical development, the United States became something other than a free society. The slave's true story, then, lies in his humane triumph over tyranny.

I first began to ponder the meaning of slavery in American history as a black schoolboy, caught by the anomaly of a slave people within a free society and by the consistent disparity between the principles of American liberty and the experience of blacks in the United States. Those early concerns brought me to this present work. I have spent nearly ten years now in a careful study of the surviving records of slaves and of those who were their masters, of free blacks and whites whose lives and thoughts were affected by slavery. As I worked, the conviction grew that there was a faulty assumption in those original concerns. The United States was a slave society; that much is certain. Whether it has, nonetheless, been a free society remains to be proved.

My aim in this book is far more modest than that, however. I wish to describe an intricate social fabric through which were woven strands of unfreedom and deliberate oppression, without which the whole would have unraveled. Taking up those strands, I hope to show something of the character of those who were slaves, especially of the integrity that gave them coherence and meaning as a people.

Focusing on their ordeal of oppression and enslavement, I have wanted to touch wherever possible the emotional and spiritual essence of their experience. That has brought me to choose a style, often evocative and impressionistic, which departs from the conventional descriptive and analytical exposition of standard histories. Through that choice, I have wanted to bring the reader closer to the minds and hearts of a people who had to endure and make choices under conditions and circumstances which are outside our experience to know.

Without this style, what I want the reader to understand might prove elusive. I have, however, in this approach risked some distortion. In describing the African experience, for example, I have presented a model, something of an archetype. The reader, of course, should know that it is impossible to reduce all of West African experience in the seventeenth and eighteenth centuries to a single model. There were hundreds of different peoples in the region from which Afro-Americans were drawn. Some were matriarchal, others patriarchal; some were monogamous, others polygynous. While the village as I describe it was the ideal African social context, it was not, in fact, ubiquitous at any moment; nor was it stable and unchanging. Peoples were forced to move, for instance, and families obliged to resettle themselves.

It is not my intent to draw a picture of a fixed and idyllic world that was shattered by foreign intrusions; rather, it is to evoke what I believe to have been the psychological and spiritual sense of order and place that was destroyed by the slave trade. There is an essential validity to that understanding. The truth that I hope the reader to know is the African captives' common sense of loss.

I have called those captives subjects of tyranny. Though tyranny is a word that few Americans would apply to our nation's history, I merely follow the Founding Fathers' understanding of that word. To them a government that was a tyranny did not rest on the consent of the governed, did not honor a person's natural rights to life, liberty, and property. They drafted "bills of rights" to protect themselves against tyranny. People must be free to speak, gather together, and share their ideas and opinions. They should worship as they please. Their persons and effects should be free from arbitrary search and seizure. Accused of crime, they should get a speedy trial by an impartial jury; and if convicted, they should not be subject to cruel and unusual punishment.

By their own standards, the governments they designed would tyrannize black people, slave and free, as well as whites who would champion their cause. That the Founding Fathers may not have admitted to tyranny matters very little. Like most white Americans, they were pleased with the results of their labors. Anyway, as John C. Calhoun in his defense of slavery was to point out, a government is no less a tyranny because a majority finds it convenient.

To call our society by its proper name requires a radical reversal of perspective. Rather than the onus of slavery falling on those who were oppressed by it, we must find out how the liberty of some Americans rested on the unfreedom of others. Rather than reiterate the obvious—that black men and women would (and did) give their lives for liberty—we must honor those who abided yet salvaged their humanity, transmitting through the generations a rich cultural and spiritual heritage.

It is not that we would give less respect to Gabriel Prosser, Denmark Vesey, and Nat Turner; nor can we say enough of the importance of Harriet Tubman and the many thousands who "voted with their feet" for freedom. Rather, it is my intent to reach for the heart of a people whose courage was in their refusal to be brutes, in their insistence on holding themselves together, on acting, speaking, and singing as men and women. For the majority of Afro-Americans did that. Their lives were not marked by extraordinary acts of defiance. They lived and they died as captives within a system of slave labor. But they produced worlds of music, poetry, and art. They reshaped a Christian cosmology to fit their spirits and their needs, transforming American Protestantism along the way. They produced a single people out of what had been many. Some of their progeny would be giants: Harriet Tubman, Sojourner Truth, Frederick Douglass, Booker T. Washington, Mary McLeod Bethune, and Ned Cobb ("Nate Shaw"). They would evoke W. E. B. Du Bois's homage in *The Souls of Black Folk*, James Weldon Johnson's in

"O Black and Unknown Bards." Their ordeal, and their dignity throughout it, speaks to the world of the indomitable human spirit.

We have continued, nonetheless, to try to prove that slaves had *manly* courage and fought for their liberty. Thomas Wentworth Higginson's statement in 1858 should have been the final word on that. He told his readers of black men and women who braved the lonely swamp, starved on prairies, clung to locomotives, rode hundreds of miles while cramped in boxes, head downward "equally near to death if discovered or deserted," who returned voluntarily to risk it all again for the sake of a wife or child. Higginson asked his readers, "What are we pale faces, that we should claim a rival capacity with theirs for heroic deeds?"

Certainly, adventures more breathtaking than all the sagas of the West, human sacrifices more moving than Iron Curtain melodramas, were the true tales of slaves and free blacks. If our histories, literature, and popular culture have not discovered this lore, it is perhaps because we have been unwilling to call oppression by its proper name.

Within that tyranny, looking beyond the acts of defiance, rebellion, and escape, we will find a quality of courage still unsung. It is in the triumph of the human spirit over unmitigated power. It raised no banners. It gained no vengeance. It was only the pervasive and persistent will among Afro-Americans to hold together through deep trauma and adversity. Much that was in their circumstance would have reduced them to brutes, to objects in the market. It would have been easy to become what many whites insisted they were: dumb, slow, insensitive, immoral, wanting in true human qualities. But slaves laid claim to their humanity and refused to compromise it, creating families where there would have been none, weaving a cosmology and a moral order in a world of duplicity, shaping an art and a world of imagination in a cultural desert.

It is exactly this triumph of the human spirit over adversity that is the great story in Afro-American slavery. It is why slaves, in their art, in their story properly understood, in their faith in themselves and their God, have been a source of inspiration to all who have come to know of them. It is why the spirituals had universal appeal—beauty, yes, but from a people who would have been crushed.

Many slaves lived their lives without much that we would call resistance. They died whole persons nevertheless, able in their souls to meet their God without shame. No black American, and certainly no white American, has cause to apologize for them. Modern history knows of no more glorious story of the triumphant human spirit.

BLACK
ODYSSEY

1

African Beginnings:
The Seamless Web

THE AFRICANS who were to become Americans came
from a region of West Africa that fanned from its
westernmost tip, around the Senegal River, south and
east, along the Bight of Benin, and south again below
the Congo River to include a region we now call Angola. Hardly a people living within this vast region,
stretching inland for two to three hundred miles, was
unrepresented in the creation of the Afro-American
people. Bambara, Fulani, Mandinka, and Wolof from
the Senegambia, the collection of peoples from Dahomey called Whydahs, the Ashanti, Coromantees,
Fanti, Ga, Hausa, Ibo, Yoruba, Angola—they all came,
like migrants from Europe and later from Asia, to mix
their seed and substance in the making of the American
and his civilization.

It was a treacherous and awful journey from whatever point they started, down the coast, through the
unimaginably inhuman Atlantic crossing, into American
slavery. Nor was that journey vast and torturous merely
in physical distance and bodily pain. Those who were

forced to make it traversed worlds of mind and spirit, leaving what they were and becoming the forebears of a people yet to be. Each man, woman, and child made that internal journey alone; but collectively, their odyssey is one of the great epics of modern times.

Some who started did not make it. Disease, frailty, brutality, and suicide took a heavy toll. But those whose way was stopped short for whatever reason will not hold us long, for ours is the story of those who endured, whether due to strength or chance or will to survive or abject surrender. They were the people who would become Afro-Americans.

Those whose origins were farthest inland came to the coast in coffles—caravans of fettered humanity—or by war canoe on the major rivers that cut deep into the African continent: the Senegal, Gambia, Niger, and the Congo—avenues over which slave raiders reached into the heartland among peoples who would never otherwise have known either the grandeur of those rivers, coursing hundreds of miles and spilling into the ocean, or the ocean itself.

Others came from among peoples closer to the coast, where disorder and tribal weakness made them easy prey for neighbors looking for people to trade.

Brought together in the dungeons of the coastal slave castles—Gorée, Elmina, Cape Coast—or the corral-like barracoons of Bonny and Calabar, they were a mélange of peoples. They might seem to have little in common save color. Yet even that sameness—given the shades of blacks and browns—was remarkable only in that they shared in not being white. One who would search out one of his own would not attend to color. He would rather listen to language, the special inflections that were his and no other's, and he would look for those familiar tribal markings and mannerisms he knew as his own. There were countless distinctions that loomed large. Yet whatever their real or imagined differences, great or small, the progeny of these Africans were to lose all vestiges of tribal difference, making one people and giving ironic validity to a coming nation's slogan: *e pluribus unum.*

Whatever his people and from wherever he came, the African was first a part of a village. The village, a collection of family compounds organized around agriculture and trade, was the center of life and comprised his world.

Nature was the throb of the village's heart. Whether its people be simple farmers of rice, yams, or groundnuts; whether they cull the rivers and coastal waters for fish; whether they be herdsmen or artisans—makers and weavers of cloth, wood-carvers, or bronze-casters—the fundamental pulses of nature—the rains, the seasons, the tides—punctuated life. Thus, each place had a sameness, a common imperative pulling all together to an insistent command that was above and beyond the individual self, the family, or the clan.

The village was the expression of the need to hold together for existence. Isolation was unthinkable. Alone, awesome nature was a threat rather than a blessing. Alone, one was helpless before all that was unknown. The smallest thing could threaten the isolated person— the elements, inanimate objects, animals, and above all, other people.

Besides, alone, a person was nobody. The self was defined in relationship to others. One was a son, a daughter, a parent, or a grandparent, and had a place, large or small, in the village. What one was known to be rested on others. One shared the reputations of kin. A wastrel or cowardly brother was one's own shame; a relation who brought glory to himself was one's own

pride. The kinsman whose name one bore shared force
and qualities of character. Each was thus tied with
others, past and present, and each was linked through
family to others in the village. The bloodlines and associations that made up the village were a finely spun
web, firmly and distinctly linking all together. The self,
who one was, was of the village. What one was to become was of the village as well.

The families and clans that located themselves together, forming the village, gave over to those chosen
or assumed wise the ultimate power for the maintenance
of order. As elders, they were respected because they
were the living repository for community experience.
Only those who lived long could contain within their
memory precedents that would serve to unravel complicated knots of dispute.

Ideally, each family settled its problems within itself.
When death set women or children adrift, the family
provided an anchor. When there was a confusion of
rights and duties, the family was expected to find its
own accord. When children or old people were without
proper care, the family would seek a just solution. But
sometimes such matters did not rest quietly within the
family, or there were disputes that caused one family to
confront another without agreement, or crises posed
dangers to all; then it was the collective judgment and
wisdom of the village, through its elders, its chief, or
council, which provided the ultimate sanction and
brought each person to know and to do what was expected.

While each served and in turn was served by the
commonwealth of the village, there was no assumption
of equality. Chiefs, elected or hereditary, leaders,
chosen or assumed, elders, patriarchs, matriarchs, com-

manded respect and gave respect in rightful order. One's age, experience, and resourcefulness could make one superior to others, obliging proper deference from them. One went on one's knees before father, mother, or elder. That being said, however, in the typical village there was little to distinguish one person or family from another in the way of material possessions and standard of living. The village did not support extremes of wealth and want.

The African was thus in a living web of interrelationships wherein personality was defined, and the possibilities of growth or change circumscribed. His character reflected his membership in an age group, clan, and family. He learned to understand and appreciate patterns that had endured for centuries and were but slightly changed over generations. The important relationships of life were controlled by a rigid etiquette learned through ritual, routine, and religion, occupying everyone and touching everything. Little of his thought was toward innovation. Age-old problems of farming, health, and warfare were solved by traditional means, or they persisted unsolved.

In the course of his life, he may have become especially honored by his people for some particular achievement or trait of character. But his real meaning lay in the fact of his "being," that he existed and "fit" where he did in the network of tribal relationships. As the reason for village was not questioned and need not be explained, he, too, was justified by the simple fact that he *was*. Since his goals and those of the village were the same—to exist—"progress" was not something he thought about.

One might say the village was the family writ large, so intimate and pervasive were its influences. Indeed, given the intricacies of blood ties and kinship, it was difficult to be precise about the margins of family as the lines attenuated outward.

The inner regions of family were sharply enough defined. Were you born into this world of relations, you would have found yourself centered in your mother's house with her other children, your brothers and sisters. But likely there would be near at hand other women, like your mother, the other wives of your father; their children, your half-brothers and half-sisters, like you, from the same father's seed. At the core of this universe would stand your father, whose greatness was in the produce of his land and his loins, whose greatest wealth was in his children. There would be a senior wife, who stood above the other women in authority. Then there would be the co-wives, with your mother and all the children ranging in age from infancy to adulthood. In such a compound, your network of relationships would begin, radiating outward to uncles and aunts, cousins, nieces and nephews. Beyond the compound and beyond the village would be others, tied to you by bloodlines, and others more remote but family nonetheless. Each such link had its discrete meaning, conferring upon the other person clear responsibilities to you and obliging you in turn.

Family compounds also housed persons who were neither of the father's nor the mother's blood. They belonged to the father because they had been captured, given as an honor by a chief, or held as a pawn in place of debt. These "slaves," as they were called, sometimes represented several generations in that status, for the custom was that a female slave's children were slaves also. As slaves, they might be servile or highly responsible persons, depending on their talents and character. They worked in the family's interest, were obedient to its authority, and might merge into the family through marriage. They were slaves only in the sense that they were held by the family. According to tradition, they could not be sold: they were not items of commerce.

The family was an economic unit, each member contributing to the whole. There was room for each to expend his energy and talent; no one was surplus. The rationale that underlay birth and nurture and training and succor was that the whole family would be harnessed to the tides of nature, that it might bring forth its fruits in abundance for the well-being of all.

Each wife had something that was hers—her land to cultivate, her chickens, her goats—which came to her when she consented to be wife to her husband. While the single end of the family's efforts was to provide the means by which to live, there might well be more than a family could eat or use. That surplus, which came from the woman's land, was hers to trade for what she wanted but did not have.

The woman went to market in her village or in the principal village nearby. Carrying her yams, peppers, groundnuts, or other produce, she would find a spot to await the right exchange. She might want poultry, hogs, goats, cloth, utensils, or whatever she could not raise or make herself. Since all the women at the market had much the same things to barter, it could be a long wait. But time was plentiful, and the market alive with news and tales of other villages. Sometimes, when nothing to exchange was found, she would take cowrie shells or other such money and await a better occasion when there would be goods to trade more to her liking.

Trading meant exchanging what one had for what one needed or desired, and the skill was in knowing the true value of both. Ideally, an exchange was made when there was a matching of value for value. The woman could then return justly proud of a well-matched trade, but shame would be on her if she gave a great deal for little. There was much room for individual skills and shrewdness. Some women did better than others, and the rewards of their industry and cunning would be reflected in the well-being of their children.

In the economy of the village, the welfare of all was far too important to allow crucial decisions to be made in personal and private ways. Thus, when to plant and harvest, when to cut and burn the fields, even what crops to plant, were matters of consensus rather than individual judgment. Not that these questions were raised each year, or much at all. Rather, the logic and intelligence of experience had locked such matters into routine behavior, so that, except for crisis or disaster, questions of choice never rose to the level of conscious, deliberate decision making.

If disaster did strike—if nature, despite the combined knowledge of villagers and elders, despite all the supplications and offerings, was too ungiving for too many seasons; if strange people moved too close, bringing violence and death—it was the unit of the family together with the unit of the village that decided what should be done.

As the welfare of each person was so intimately linked to that of the whole family, the village, and the tribe, and all in turn rested on the person, no important decision was really personal. Surely, the matter of marriage and the augmentation of family could not be left to the judgment of young people. Kin and clan would assure that mating served both the young and all those who must, in time, depend upon the young. The young man acquired from his family (or, more likely, from the substance of his own labor) bridal dues, which he would give to the family of the woman to be his wife.

The couple would then establish their household, according to custom, near the bride's or the groom's family, keeping the growing unit a close-knit fabric.

For a person to be one of many was no strange thing, for from the time the child left the back of his mother and started to walk on his own, he was among others and dependent on them. Older boys and girls cared for him and taught him the intricate social interplay of child society.

The child moved through stages of life together with others his age, all learning and experiencing the same quality of life. Before them were older children and adults in whose existence was clearly calibrated the stages of one's own development; behind were younger children, already one's charge and responsibility, whose almost every rough way one had already mastered. This made even children sense the rightness of the unalterable association between age and wisdom.

All that need be learned was, in time, before one's eyes—the mysteries of the body, birth, life, death—all to be seen and explained. As a girl grew, she was pulled more closely into marriage, pregnancy, and the birth of others, until her own time came.

A boy could watch with silent awe as his elder brothers went through secret rites from which they emerged with the marks of the tribe and a far-away look, as if they had seen into the most distant darkness. But it would be another year or two until his own time would come. Then he, too, would know the exquisite agony of the boy-man/man-child rite and confront enigmas that would stay with him forever. But he could look into the eyes of the others who had shared that moment, as they had shared all moments from leaving their mother's arms. They could look at each other and know their oneness.

It was a special way of life, being so intimately tied to others, being so defined in terms of community. But the links that bound all together went beyond the compounds of the village and clan to the villages of the tribe. So, even when one went to neighboring villages, one was never a stranger. Through the kin of mother, father, uncles, and aunts, there was family and welcome. One was not likely to wander far from one's village, but wherever one went within the tribe, one was a person—the son or daughter of a person—related to someone known. The web of relationships extended far and gave one a sense of place and certainty. But it tied one to obligations and duties, and made the concept of individual freedom the fantasy of a lunatic.

It was right that one's destiny was of the group. For what one was, was of the whole. Had it not been told and justified in the lives of those who had lived longer? Was not one tied to them in experience, just as they had been tied to their fathers before them, and their fathers to those who had sired them, right back to the fathers of the tribe? The present, where one stood in time, was a natural extension of all time and experience to that moment. One was a creature of a history that verified the rightness of things as they were; the lessons of human experience seemed so invariable, changing when they did by infinitesimal shifts of practice and habit.

Lest one lose sight of that experience or miscalculate its weight, it was wound in an endless skein of history, told in stories hardly varying with each telling or in long narrative songs, which located each moment in its rightful place. Each person was made part of that historical strand and could find his way back to people and family no longer alive, to times and events before the actual recollection of even the oldest one present. One's family, details of personal character and achievement, lived in those songs and stories. Through them, one was lifted into the importance of one's birthright and made to share the greatness of his people and their past, beyond remembered time.

Such history, therefore, was tribal and familial, but it was also personal. Who one was, where one came from, what one was expected to be, the heights of courage and character that were to be achieved, were woven into the fabric that linked one's self to all, touching, at last, the first father of the tribe, the one who, through superhuman power and character, had pulled together the people in the birth of the tribe itself.

When one imagined the first fathers of the tribe, one had gone beyond mere history and touched upon the beginning of existence itself, for they were almost god-like. It was as if life itself had spun a web of infinite intricacy, beginning with the tribal fathers, tying all together and linking everything to the present self. Death mattered not. It was a mere punctuation. Life was of the person, and the person of life—all a continuum—so that the forces of life ebbed and flowed through him, making him a conduit of the life force. Dead or alive, he continued to impress on life the energy of his own spirit and character.

Was it not possible in time of need to call to those since departed the living, who in their time had overcome such troubles? And was it not, in merely recollecting them, that one could feel the power of those who had overcome their trials? And was it not that inspiration that made one find, within himself, the resources to overcome one's own troubles?

Life was all there was; not good and evil alone, but good and evil bound together in a mélange too complex to comprehend. When all one's easiest efforts came to fruition in bounty beyond expectations, that was the force of life working through the individual, multiplying the force of his own will and character. Doubtless, ancestors long since dead had brought their own force of character to his enterprise. But, on the other hand, when the best that one could do in mind, heart, and body led to meager and insubstantial results, that too was life's force in its diminished form. Chances were that people and spirits unfriendly to him had gained ascendance, and thus, for him, the tide was at ebb.

While a European might think of evil as an element of moral corruption, sin, and personal culpability, the African was more likely to see evil as a natural part of the hand he was dealt. Evil came to him, as to all in their turn. One's best defense was respect for traditional obligation and the strength of personal character. Still, despite every plan and precaution, there was the unexpected—the joker in the deck. Thus the painful reminder that the life force, which had spun the web that made the person and all he knew, was at last an unfathomable mystery.

One could never forget one's helplessness before the great rush and surge of life. Thus, as each morsel of food and drink one took was accepted, one's ancestors were remembered. One poured "libations" into the earth, thanking and invoking spirits and ancestors. One called them by name to share his substance so that they would be remembered and at home in his house, so that they would never leave him, especially in time of need.

The force of life that tied person to person and to all time past linked a person as well to all things. The force that moved through him moved through plants of the field, trees, animals, and even stones. Spirits dwelt in each thing and imparted to it special character. Did not the fields throb with that spirit, sometimes flushing full and plentiful, sometimes waning meager, as that life force surged or slept within?

The spirit that dwelt within each thing had its own character, its own force to be expressed. Out of the wood it came to command the wood-carver's hand to make itself manifest. The spirit of the wood, the stone, the clay, possessed the artisan to its own ends as much as the artisan expressed himself. One was fortunate and gifted if one could make oneself the instrument of those spirits that lurked within all things.

Ritual and ceremonial observation attended almost every event of the village and family. The engagement of all in a vortex of music, dance, and celebration lifted the events of birth, marriage, and death to cosmic significance.

The whole of the community joined together to create that electric atmosphere in which the world of palpable reality and the world of spirit would be as one: each the instrument and the effect of the other—will beyond will, consciousness beyond awareness, thought beyond mind. Each person within his place played a role but understood himself only through the whole; like a member of a secret society, each was linked to others by the mysteries that made them one. All moving, as would sometimes appear, along no single thread or to no command. But the multiple rhythms and apparent chaos of movement would, like life itself, come to focus in the singularity of the most intense pulse of common ecstasy.

The drums sustained a relentless beat, flutes and voices spun an intricate pattern of sound through the rhythms. The bodies of dancers turned and twisted and spun within that music like tall blades of grass within the fingers of the wind. Dancers' feet beat out the pulse of spirit against the earth; beads hissed, and bells and metal rang with each movement of the body. Dancers and drums and flutes and voices were all instruments of the same music and rhythms, playing against and with one another to quicken the electric spark that moved them, until the atmosphere, too heavy to hold itself stable, would clap with the thunder and flash with the glory of the spirits' presence among them.

Some special person—special because his nerves were attuned as no others were—would be invaded and "possessed" by a spirit. An animal to be sacrificed—goat or chicken—worked out the anguish of his pain and death through the surrogate human body. When the spirit of such an animal, or rain or wind or the generative force of the earth took possession of the body of doctor, priest, or priestess, such a chosen one moved no longer to a rhythm and design of his own. Rather, like a leaf in a high, turbulent wind he gyrated with dizzying convulsive starts, until finally the spirit had departed, and he lay spent and empty.

The African's personal world, then, was both private and cosmic. Nothing he was or did or that affected him was too small to be woven into the fabric of all being. And, equally, nothing was so abstract, so divine, so sacred, as not to touch him in an immediate and direct way. His was a self-contained world that would account for all he would be expected to confront. His place in his world was defined neatly and carefully through his relationships. His sense of person and purpose was sustained by the spiritual ambience that encapsulated his people. His world had its comforts. While the room it left for mystery was infinite, there was little, if any, place for doubt.

Yet, it was no Eden, no paradise, from which he was to be expelled. As much as his world view took into

account life as a dynamic and mysterious forc
not comprehend change coming from outside the
work it assumed. Status, stability, and order we
values; change was unwanted and, thus, unprepared .or.
So, the African's world was especially vulnerable to
shocks and jolts from outside an order whose principal
strength was its parochial neatness.

At best, life was not unmitigated sweetness. The
spirits of nature and life were fickle partners and com-
panions. Seldom did they behave as expected. They
were not to be taken for granted; they required constant
attention and cajoling. And, sometimes, power fell into
the wrong hands—those who would bend an individual
to their will. Then he would have to bend lower under
a burden that had once been light but now broke the
back.

Rather than being an existence of pastoral simplicity,
African life was characterized by strong contrasts. Because the routines of daily living were flat and continuous, the special occurrence hit with more telling impact. One sensed in the purest form the extremes of
suffering and joy, adversity and happiness. Lacking an
array of instruments for planned dullness, the African's
pleasure was ecstasy, but his pain was absolute agony.
Except for plateaus of routine living, the African would
experience both.

Without assumptions of change and plans for exigencies, calamities and affliction fell harder on the African
family and village than they would on people today.
Droughts, floods, or raids that would claim a year's produce could mean total devastation, followed by starvation and death for nearly everyone. One was either in
good health, and illness was the threshold of death.

The senses were honed to sharpness. The wetness of
rain, the coldness of night, the warmth of the sun, the

hotness of fire, the blackness of the night's sky, the brilliance of stars and moon, were unmitigated sensations. We can have little sense of the keenness with which food, drink, and dance were enjoyed.

Where, as in some African societies, there was a regal and noble caste, one could see it in the sparkle of gold and bronze ornaments, one could feel it in the difference between royal cloth and that worn by ordinary people. In such richness and power, rank and order were distinguished by pomp, which was heralded by proud or cruel publicity. The great chiefs never moved without glorious displays of arms and attendants, exciting fear and envy. Such richness and power were the more pronounced because of the plainness of everything else.

It is as one senses the emotive force of such contrasts, such purity of sensation, that one can comprehend the power of the chants, the music, the dance, the processions that attended funerals, births, marriages, executions, and all notable events. It was not merely these grand events that were raised by the sacredness of ceremony to the rank of mysteries, but incidents of less importance—a journey, a task, a visit—were equally attended by a thousand formalities, benedictions, and ceremonies. As one senses the explosive force of such contrasts, one can feel the impact of the start of rain after the dry months, a sudden fire in the darkness of the night, voices chanting in unison, the sharp report of drums splintering the air, the sudden violence of warriors sweeping down, shattering the calm of village life.

Whatever the neatness and completeness of the African's social fabric and cosmology, there was a general feeling of insecurity because one was subject to the unknown, and swings of events provided vast contrasts, not finely calibrated shifts and changes. One could easily fall victim to the unknown or to the chronic form that wars might take. So one turned in everlasting fear to gods, doctors, and priests.

The African's world did not prepare him for the onrush of history, which would sweep him out of familiar and accustomed settings into an experience beyond imagination. Even those who were not to be unraveled from the social fabric were to have their lives altered and suffer the dominance of an alien hand. Like all parochial contexts, that of the Africans fostered an ironic self-satisfaction, which would make them inattentive to the dangers of real change when it came.

At first, the agents of change were innocuous enough. From the fifteenth century, the Portuguese, Spanish, Dutch, French, and English began to arrive. Like African peoples, they were different men, speaking different tongues, hostile to one another—but all European, pale-skinned, and Christian. From the first, they wanted to trade: gold, ivory, and similar precious things; but, also, they traded for men. These outlanders built strong points along the coast at Elmina, Cape Coast, Gorée Island, Dixcove, and the like in order to protect themselves and their trade from others like themselves. And they were quick to warn the neighboring Africans of the evil and treacherousness of other white men who spoke in other tongues.

Where they could not erect forts, they came with their boats up the rivers as far as they dared, or they stayed with their boats off the coast, to trade with those onshore. Who would fear such men, always at one another's throats fighting and killing, so quick to go down on their knees and offer any deference so as to affect their trade, whose miserable feebleness caused them to die so fast that they counted themselves lucky to survive

six months or a year? Who could be worried about men
who were ignorant of the land beyond the coast, who
were uninformed about the ways of inland peoples, and
who, thus, must be forever dependent on the superior
knowledge of Africans? To the African mind, the European might come and go, but the familiar and traditional world would remain constant.

The Europeans did continue to come, though seldom
penetrating beyond the coast, always merely seeking
trade. However, in the sixteenth, seventeenth, and eighteenth centuries, as their colonial empires expanded in
the Americas, the trade that they sought came to focus
more exclusively on human beings. The African merchants who were their trading partners were more and
more pressed to supply men, women, and children to
the insatiable craw across the seas.

The twentieth-century Western mind is frozen by the
horror of men selling and buying others as slaves and
even more stunned at the irony of black men serving as
agents for the enslavement of blacks to whites. Shocking
though it is, this human barter was truly the most stark
representation of what modernism and Western capitalist expansion meant to traditional peoples. In the
New World, people became items of commerce, their
talents, their labors, and their produce thrown into the
marketplace, where their best hope was to bring a decent price. The racial irony was lost on African merchants, who saw themselves as selling people other than
their own. The distinctions of tribe were more real to
them than race, a concept that was yet to be refined by
nineteenth- and twentieth-century Western rationalists.

Beyond the shock of the obvious, the crucial matter
is that the world of the African merchant allowed him
to see only his limited involvement. Had he been able
to perceive the vast enterprise in which he was a crucial

element, had he been able to calculate the enormous wealth that was to be produced by the hands of those he traded, had he—like a common market-woman—weighed accurately the comparative values, he would have demanded a different exchange from that which he received. But nothing in the world he knew could prepare him for such a judgment.

African merchants, and chiefs who acted as merchants, had about them the fantastic aura of the caliph of *The Arabian Nights*. Their wealth and power being personal, not societal, were manifested in anger, covetousness, and cupidity. Wealth's power mirrored personal pride and could be reflected both in the ceremonial reverence of others—such as the obeisance paid in kneeling and touching one's forehead to the ground—and in the continued accumulation of material possessions. To have wealth, to use it, to destroy it, were all symbols of power, and it was either in luxury and dissipation or in gross avarice that wealth and power were enjoyed most.

The Europeans with whom they traded, however, had a different calculus of value. Capitalists all, they made a distinction between a simple thing and one that produces other things, that creates wealth. There was for them a different kind of wealth—spectral and inpalpable—founded on credit and investment.

So the Europeans traded guns, ammunition and powder, pots and pans, beads and cloth, to the African merchants, receiving in exchange men, women, and children, who had within them the capacity to produce wealth. Whenever the African merchants were dissatisfied, they demanded, and generally got, more of the same for what they offered. It was a bad trade no matter how much they received, for after the rum, the powder, and the bullets had been spent, they found themselves dependent upon their European trading partners for additional supplies. But on the other side, the humanity that was sold out of Africa was destined to build wealth as well as an empire, turning erstwhile trading partners into colonial lords and masters. It was much too late before the African tradesmen learned the first principle of the African market-women: it is not important what the thing you hold is worth to you; you must know what its real value is to the person who wants to trade for it.

Supposing the African's world had prepared him to see more, it still might not have prevented the trade of Africans as slaves. But, perhaps, it would have made the merchant get a better bargain, compensating Africa in some constructive way for the drain in intelligence, skills, and regenerative wealth that was siphoned off in the course of the slave trade.

In fact, however, there was little that might have been changed, given the European contact. No African peoples along the coast had the power to control all of the trade. Lacking the ability to provide a united front against the innocuous European merchants, each African merchant or chief was obliged either to trade or be excluded.

The trade in people, of course, was not unfamiliar to them. Tribes had raided other tribes to gain space or dominance over a region. Captives of such wars had long been taken as slaves, some of whom could be traded away. The thought, then, that a person could be captive, owned, or traded was not repulsive.

The African peoples whom the Europeans contacted along the coast—what is now the Ivory Coast, Dahomey, Liberia, Ghana, Nigeria, and Zaire—were the weakest and most disorganized in West Africa. Most of them had moved there, fleeing the power of the more forceful and organized inland peoples. But the contact with Europeans and the trade in guns gave them a technological advantage.

The process was circular and insidious. Guns empowered otherwise weak peoples to raid and capture others for trade to the Europeans. The raids forced others to procure guns to protect themselves, and that meant selling what the Europeans wanted: human beings. So, in time, all were drawn into the trade, and each had to remain in it to maintain power.

All the while the Africans could play the Europeans off, one against the other, as at Elmina, where the local chiefs would support the Dutch, then the Danes, then the British. But never were the Africans able to be done with them because they had become dependent on what only the Europeans could provide: guns.

This trade and contact with Europeans disrupted African life in more ways than are apparent from the slave trade alone. The force of change was beyond what could be conceived by tradition. Guns gave power to persons who would not normally have wielded it, such as a merchant or chief, who could then build a personal army, making him no longer dependent on family and tribal authority. Thus, his power could become autocratic and despotic in a way uncommon in Africa.

But more than that, these forces of change rudely tore men, women, and children from the web so finely spun by traditional Africa, and it cast them out, as atoms. Each tribe in the wide region lost its share (some more, some less) to this massive, forced migration. Because tradition had no place for such a rupture, the web was knit closed again, with scarcely a trace of the wound. All that would remain would be cryptic hints in the oral histories that spun on relentlessly.

As for those who were torn away to America, none would have willed it so. None, beforehand, could have

imagined the awful agony to be endured—the separation from all that they were, the voyage into empty
space, the trials of adjustment to a new life. Rudely
forced, they were, nevertheless, destined to help create
a new world, to become the founding fathers and
mothers of a new people.

2

The Rupture
and the Ordeal

THINKING BACK on the African's capture and forced migration to America, we tend to focus on the pain and brutality, the great physical suffering, captives must have undergone. There is testimony enough to credit our wildest fantasies about the horrors and inhumanity of the slave trade—the cross-country coffles, the infamous middle passage. Or we think about the loss of freedom that defined the slave's status, imagining people, once free, who through the agency of the slaver were placed in bondage.

We are thus distracted from what is more profound and personal in the experience. We tend to see only the surface of what was, perhaps, the most traumatizing mass human migration in modern history. Pain, suffering, and brutality, much as they are feared and avoided, are part of the imagined possibilities of everyone, everywhere. Any normal social context has within it the potential for misfortune, pain, oppression, and victimization. One sees around oneself those who have fallen victim to disease or crippling accident or criminality or impoverishment. Normal existence makes one conscious of such possibilities, and therefore we become conditioned to living with such personal disaster without questioning the fundamental ground on which we stand.

But what of that catastrophe that spins one outside the orbit of the known universe, that casts one into circumstances where experience provides neither wisdom nor solace? What if the common ground one shared with the sound and the infirm, the rich and the poor, the clever and the dull, the quick and the dead, fell away and one were left isolated in private pain with no known point of reference? Would not, then, the pain itself be the slightest of miseries?

Similarly, to be unfree would of itself amount to little more than misfortune if the terms by which one lived with one's fellow men and the calculus by which one was valued remained unchanged. After all, freedom, as we think of it, is a modern Western notion—somewhat a fiction even so—and neither European nor African involved in the slave trade would have presumed freedom to have been the natural state of man. The African, certainly, and probably the European, would have questioned the desirability of a freedom that described an independent person having slight social and political restraints and responsibilities. Unfreedom, and even slavery, was conceivable to the African as a normal state of mankind. The African had even seen slaves about him, those of his father and of other men. At the worst, it was a misfortune, or sometimes a circumstance that a clever slave could work to his advantage. But the transatlantic slave trade was outside that experience; it was something radically new and unimaginable. In a process that could only be related to a witch's spell, one was transformed from person to thing.

Two edges of the slave trade—the rupture of the African from the social tissue that held all meaning for him and his conversion into a marketable object—cut the deepest and touched each to the quick. All other horrors attending to the trade were merely external and superficial cruelties. With luck they might abate in time or be mitigated by circumstance. But those two shocks reverberated to the very foundation of the African's being, changing forever the framework of his life. Thus, those few who suffered these shocks but somehow managed to escape the Atlantic crossing were so altered by the experiences, so set adrift, that they could never find their way back into the world from which they had been torn.

Such experiences do not happen with a single blow. Certainly the mind cannot take in, whole, such devastating events. Rather, as in an earthquake, which begins with tremors, building to catastrophe, each shock deeper and broader than the last, one is finally left alone among other moving creatures, stunned, wounded, and isolated amid the shambles of the known world. In such a disaster, it is impossible for the survivor to fix the point of the most telling blow and to completely rediscover himself after its enormity has passed. So, too, the African was engulfed in a process, the end of which was impossible to see from its onset and its precise beginnings lost forever to recall.

The first capture might have come suddenly, without warning. One might have traveled that way beyond the village many times before—to trade at nearby market villages or on business for the family. Always, beyond the village, in small groups or alone, the air was charged with fear and anticipation of the unexpected, for outside the known and safe precincts, the simplest task could become adventure. There had been stories enough of

people, alone, being taken by evil men who might devour them or feed them to some insatiable spirit. Men
and women were known simply to vanish without a
trace. No warning and no anticipation, however, was
sufficient to prepare for the moment when it came—
when unknown men appeared, as if from nowhere, with
awful faces and terrible noises, turned one around, beat
him to his knees, and pulled him bound and dazed along
an unknown trail into emptiness.

Or the blow may have come with more warning, one
of a series of raids on neighborhood villages by men
who seemed to want only to take people. Straggling
wanderers might have brought first word of danger,
refugees who had missed death and capture, now seeking some tattered end of family and clan to which to
attach themselves. As well, the village may have heard
drums telling of violence in the country. The village
would be electric with the tales of disaster striking so
near at hand, and children would sense the fear as it
quivered in the adult whisperings or showed in the
quick, nervous movements of heads and eyes as they
strained for the first sight or sound that would signal
the coming blow.

All the warning and expectation might mean little to
a simple farming village. The men and boys might
gather their knives and spears. But such tools and such
men were better at clearing land and killing wild beasts
than fighting off men who had become specialists in
battle. The village might seek to evoke spirits, retell the
tales of ancient glories and valiant men of the past to
awaken the dormant martial sense, to encourage the
men in the possibilities of overcoming aggression. For
had not their fathers, far before their own time, shown
the way? Yet, there might linger the suspicion—as some
would counsel—that the best thing might be to move

away, out of the path of those who raid, because like all things, this too would pass, the storm would have run its course, and life would go on as it had. Indeed, much time had passed since the last report of a raid in the neighborhood, and that was further away than the time before. Even now, the danger might well have passed.

There could never have been preparation enough when the blow finally fell. The drums may have foretold it. The nerves of all may have been stretched taut awaiting the first sign. But when the screaming, wild-faced men spilled into the village, their stick-weapons rivaling drums with their noise, fire with their smoke, and blowing down people as if by magic; when old men and women were cut down, and children ran like screeching chickens through the village streets: no warning, no preparation, could have been enough. Farmers' weapons and peasants' courage seemed feeble against the onslaught. Death and blood were all around. Huts and compounds, large and small, crackled under the torch. In the chaos that raged and swirled, some might sneak away unnoticed and fly like the wind to find a place to hide. But most would be swept up and bound together that they might watch the smoldering ruins of their lives.

Some reasoned that security and safety lay in attacking first. To sit back quietly attending fields was the way of disaster. Better to sharpen the instruments of battle and call upon martial ancestors to accompany them into war. Better to exchange their captives with those who hungered for men, exchange them for those sticks of war that blew all down before, better to be so aggressive, so formidable, so frightening, that others would not dare attack.

Such was one way to security, but it necessarily fed the monster that threatened and unsettled the land. And such forays did not always go as planned. The battle, once begun, surged in its own course. The warrior would look up to find himself separated from his fellows, isolated, with no way back. One who had sought to capture was now captive.

Or he might have been spit out from among his people. Some twist or turn in his thought had caused him to see things differently from others, had made him hold too lightly the community's proscriptions against disorder. He took things that were not properly his own. He destroyed things or sacred objects or family peace. Or his view worked so perversely against all positive force that he appeared possessed by those spirits that were against life. He, indeed, had come to feel inhabited by snakes and commanded by another will. Whatever, the village had come to believe that he was an instrument of evil forces, that recent misfortunes could be laid at his feet, that he had become a threat to public peace. Was it not better, then, to vomit up such a creature than to harbor and nurture him in one's bowels until the whole body sickened with corruption? So he, and perhaps some of his kin, would be set out on a path, the end of which no one knew.

Stolen, captured, or rejected, African men, women, and children had no means to save themselves. Pleading and crying availed not, for pity was not the issue. Promises of goods the family would exchange availed not, for these people were items worth more than the cloth or animals or things they knew to be of value. Evoking the spirits availed not, for it seemed in one act there was an emptiness where all familiar spirits had turned their backs, closed their ears. Even then, it was only a hint of what was to follow. Being captured or taken was not really to be abandoned: there remained points of reference that were familiar. They knew something of the land around and the peoples nearby. They were not really far from their own people, they would be missed, someone would come to get them. At worst, they would be taken as slaves into someone's household.

Quite often, indeed, a captive would be held for short periods in several villages along the way to the large coastal trading centers. One worked at such moments in someone's family; there was a heartening familiarity. The work and the conditions remained within the realm of the conceivable. Perhaps, from such places, one could get word to one's own people to bargain for release. Despairing in that, at least one could make the best of bad fortune, casting one's lot among a new people.

That would have been an unhappy result, but anything would be better than marching along a trail to nowhere. Each step would take one further from home, and each turn or twist would make the way back the more baffling.

One might stay in such way stations a month, no more. The time would come when he would be bound together with others, and the march would continue. After repeated stops, hope waned that the trek would ever end. Onward the road turned, meeting rivers that flowed further still. At some moment, all one's imprecations, all one's pleas to ancestors, all one's evoking of spirits, sound in the ears as the hollowness of one's own voice. At such a moment, he would sense the most dreadful meaning in what had happened. He was alone, abandoned by all he knew that could have given him support and anchor: village, family, and even his gods.

As he stumbled and was dragged across space, clues to the future came to him as fearful tales, like fantasies and wild dreams—all was possible now that this was possible: rivers so vast that there was no other side; an end to the earth where one would fall off; men whose skins were the color of plucked chickens, whose hair was as string; men like monsters who ate nothing but other men. Such tales buzzed through his head; such visions swam before his eyes.

From the beginning there were signs to tell the captive he was no longer the same. Before, he could say his name, claim his family and clan, and all would know without further explanation who he was and what weight he had among others. But now his name meant nothing to those who held him, yet he meant something to them: he was important.

He might have sensed this unknown thing in the eyes and voices of his captors. They were pleased with him; they liked him. He was young and strong. Things were upside down because the old were not honored and respected but treated like the sick and the feeble. Little was done to see that they ate or rested. Rather, they were driven along until they dropped. Then they were left to die. But all eyes were on him.

At each place when there was a changing of hands, the same flashes of understanding crossed the faces of those who brought them and those who received them. It was like in the market, where the women bargained in trade. There were the looks of depreciation, the haggling back and forth until a trade was made: "I have just so much for these you have brought, no more; that is my final price." So the captive was like a thing to be bartered in the market.

It resembled the market, yet was different, for the stranger did not look at the captive and say: "Here is just the strong one I need to clear my fields; he will meet my needs" or "Yes, this woman will serve my household properly and do my wives' bidding." Here, the buyer did not have a need of his own; rather, he sought to judge the trade in terms of a need of someone else, further on; a need that he could not fully comprehend. "*They* are paying *thus* and *so* for such a one as this," he seemed to say. He merely wanted to make the best bargain so that he, in his turn, would find the trade to his advantage.

The captive thus was dislodged not only from his accustomed place and home. He was also severed from his intrinsic value. He became an abstraction; real and tangible though he was, his meaning to others had nothing to do with the immediate, real, or essential. Little wonder he was likely to believe he would, in time, be eaten.

The sense of personal tragedy and private misfortune was diluted and washed away as one became mixed with many others. Captives like himself but different in language and manner were bound together in the coffles, which strung their agonizing way toward the coast. At the end of the long march or the cascade in war canoe, he would be stuffed and packed with countless others— nameless, now selfless others—in the dungeons of slave castles or the corral-like barracoons. All, a sea of the miserable and lost.

Like a ritual of renaming, a rite of new identity, he and the others, each in turn, were forced to kneel, and a mark or letter was burned into their flesh with a branding iron. The cry and the pain were brief, nothing new in what had become a litany of wails and moans. But the ritual symbolized a new initiation.

As far as the pain went, it was not so great as circumcision, more intense and long-lasting than that which followed scarification. But with that earlier pain, he had been brought into manhood, made to feel himself in common fellowship with his brothers and other men of the tribe. He had suffered that pain and through it found his selfhood enhanced by new status. But the fire of the brand was to burn out of him who he was and to mark him as property and a thing. Name mattered not, family mattered not, ancestral glories mattered not. He was what the mark on his shoulder said he was, a thing belonging to a company, no more and no less.

It was the company's mark, and the company had need to know how good a physical specimen it had come by. So the captives stood before white men—perhaps seeing them for the first time and finding in their skins verification for some of the rumors. The white men and their African helpers went over their bodies with attention to detail: they felt their wounds and scars, opened their mouths and noticed their teeth, looked into their noses and eyes, and passed them along. The company cared that no one who was healthy would injure or kill himself. Forced to eat if they would not, they would live despite their will. Their lives had value to the company even if they ceased to have meaning to themselves.

Anonymity seemed achieved. The rupture of the web rendered them atoms, not part of a living tissue. They had been wrenched from all ties and known things, and they had been transformed from persons into items of commerce. It merely remained for them to be packed into the bowels of ships and carried across the Atlantic, where they were destined to profit others and build an empire.

From the sixteenth century to the nineteenth, the trade would grow from a trickle to a veritable flood of men, women, and children. Gradually, the trade would change from a casual barter of persons for goods to fixed formulas and conventions. The African merchants and chiefs would always expect to haggle and to bargain for the best price, as was the African custom. The European trader would learn what ritualized obsequiousness, which gestures to power and vanity, were essential to successful trade.

The European rivals changed places from time to time. They fought among themselves and connived with African chiefs against one another. Such divisiveness and selfish bickering amused the African merchants, and they tried where they could to exploit rivalries to get a better price or to secure support against African rivals.

But such bargains and shifts in strategy mattered little to the ever-growing current of humanity that moved over the roads and rivers. Strands of despairing humanity linked together by rope or limbs of trees straggled their way through the land and through time. The technology of these caravans improved very slightly over the centuries. In time, the drivers would have guns rather than swords and spears. Great iron collars and ankle irons with long extending spokes were devised for captives so that those who might flee into the bush would be ensnared in the overgrowth. Those who would make part of the journey by river were spared, if not the fear, much of the physical exhaustion of the trek.

By trail or by canoe, the traffic became regularized over the centuries. Depending on the distance, it would take weeks or months to make the journey to the coast. By the mid-eighteenth century, one would expect such travel to be uneventful. Some captives, being too weak from age or illness or wounds, would die, of course. Some, from remorse and hopelessness, would attempt suicide; but alert guards minimized that. The despair and disorganization of the captives made insurrection and escape difficult and seldom successful, but despite the risks there were some attempts nonetheless. There were also interlopers, who might attack the caravan in transit. Such raids were risky to both the traders and the captives, for all lives were endangered and there was only the slightest chance that one could escape in the confusion.

The paths and riverways led to the great entrepôts on the coast. The Portuguese had built Elmina Castle in 1481. It was actually a fort rather than a castle, anchored on one side to the rocks coming from the sea and protected on two sides by water; consequently, the only access was a narrow spit of land, which could be easily defended. The castle changed hands several times, finally becoming an English possession in the nineteenth century. The upper floors contained the quarters of the European "governors" and officers. On the ground level were the garrisons for European soldiers, who were to protect the installation and supervise the captives. There was also room for the necessary African functionaries. For the sake of good order, however, most non-Europeans lived away from the fort.

The captives would have first seen Elmina as a great white stone edifice isolated against the sea—the first European building they had seen. They would enter over a drawbridge, which spanned the moat and opened into the large courtyard. Here, they would be assembled, inspected, branded, made to exercise, and gathered to be shipped away.

But until a boat came, it might be weeks or even months that they would wait in the dungeons of the fort. The dungeons were high, vaulted rooms, guarded by iron gates, the only source of air and light being narrow slit windows. In the darkness the captives would not see the countless bats that covered the ceilings, but they would hear their cries and the rush of their wings. Surely, all the spirits of darkness had assembled in that place to feed the agony.

Elmina was little different from the other entrepôts. La Maison des Esclaves, in the harbor at Dakar, was smaller, as were Dixcove, Fort Metal Cross, and Cormantyne. But the nearby Cape Coast Castle was much larger; the captives marched down a steep incline deep underground, where their dungeon was a dark cavern cut into the natural rock. Tens of thousands of black pilgrims to the New World passed this way, leaving beads and artifacts behind, sweat and tears, seeping into the last ground of Africa they would know.

The great stock pens, called barracoons, at the Niger delta ports had both the advantages and disadvantages of being out of doors. There was air enough, and there was not the sense of interment in dungeons. But the sun and rain, once sweet and sustaining, were enervating to the crouched, half-naked crowd.

All such places—the Europeans called them factories —were fitted for the single enterprise of collecting, evaluating, sorting, consigning, and shipping people to America. These goods had to be protected from self-inflicted injury, which would lower their value, and fed at a minimal cost that would still sustain life and health adequately enough to command a good price. Here were the first principal manifestations of modern, mercantile capitalism on the west coast of Africa. Through the gates of these places was to pass the principal export of West Africa for over two centuries: the human stock essential to New World wealth.

Those who managed these commodities in trade wanted to judge them on the grounds of efficiency and profit. Questions of morality or ethics or feelings for fellow human creatures necessarily confounded considerations of how best to pack a boat with human cargo. The European merchants and factotums who made these judgments steeled themselves against sentimentality; or, rather, the natural selection that found suitable men for this work would automatically exclude those who might have moral qualms.

The conditions of transoceanic travel were never good during the Atlantic slave trade. The ships were small, seldom larger than 350 tons. During most of the period, the general understanding of navigation and the technology of sailing were skimpy enough to make all voyages risky. The crews of ships, mainly drawn from the margins of European life, were themselves working under duress and suffering conditions of work little better than the captives in the holds. Under the best of circumstances, therefore, these ships sailed close to the edge of peril. There were, of course, the standard hazards of sailing vessels: storms and calms. There was also, particularly during the years of the most intense mercantile competition, the risk that a vessel, with its slave cargo, might fall into the hands of hostile adventurers. Alternately, the densely packed ships might be swept with disease—aggravated and intensified by overlong delays due to calms or misadventure. In either case, much of the human cargo would be thrown into the sea to prevent capture or disease.

For those who ventured their lives and capital in the slave trade, it was a risky enterprise that exacted a heavy toll in money and lives, European as well as African. It offered, however, substantial wealth to those who profited. There would be many a family fortune and industrial empire whose foundations in capital accumulation would rest on the trade in slaves. At the height of the trade, healthy young African men could be bought for as low as ten dollars in Africa and sold for as much as six hundred dollars in America. While these figures represent extremes, they illustrate the magnitude of profit that could be gained from a cargo of two or three hundred captives.

Those Europeans who remained in Bristol or Liverpool, Brest or Amsterdam, Salem or Boston or Newport, might hazard only money and ships. Those who, by choice or compulsion, manned the ships or administered the trade from Africa, placed in jeopardy their health and their lives. Navigational risks were standard to all trade, but the special nature of this merchandise also introduced the possibilities of slave uprisings and contagion due to epidemic disease spawned in congested holds.

Wherever Europeans and Africans met, they exchanged diseases. European sailors brought gonorrhea and syphilis and measles, while Africans carried various forms of fevers, including yellow fever and malaria, amoebic dysentery, and other tropical ills. The immunities and defenses against known microorganisms were of little avail against new strains. Within the slave-ship incubators, microbes, viruses, and parasites survived better than men and women. A voyage of normal length could be expected to take its human toll, but when there was mischance or delays, short rations reduced human resistance even further. The losses could be devastating.

To the ship's captain (often an investor), the problems were clear enough, even if the solutions were not. He would be certain, even in a problemless crossing, to lose some slaves. Would it be better to take on as many slaves as his ship could hold or to find some optimum capacity that would calculate profit on a greater rate of survival? On the one hand, the captain would be willing to risk a high percentage of loss on the assumption that the numbers actually landed alive would more than make up for those who perished. On the other hand, he could assume that a less packed vessel and more tolerable conditions would reduce to a negligible figure the loss in middle passage, making the voyage more efficient. From the captain's point of view, it was risky either way, but the odds tended to favor those who chose to cover every available inch of space with human merchandise. This was especially true since much of the loss at sea could be recompensed to the investors by insurance, whereas there would be no return for the space that was not filled at the outset.

In addition to the general practice of filling all available space, attempts were made to create room where none had existed before. Thus, Africans were shackled and made to lie "spoonlike" on platforms built in the holds of small ships. The holds were about five feet from deck to overhead, with six-foot-wide platforms dividing the space. A ship's capacity was a matter of ingenuity and callous inhumanity. The English Parliament in 1788, attempting to reform practices of overcrowding, restricted the capacity to three slaves for every two tons of ship. In the celebrated illustration of the *Brookes*, we get a sense of what those proportions meant, when 451 slaves would be packed on a ship weighing 320 tons.

Unlike the experience of the European immigrants crossing the Atlantic, time and technology did not serve to make the Africans' passage easier. The British decision in 1807 to outlaw the slave trade and to patrol the African coast coincided with the end of the legal importation of slaves into the United States. But these curtailments only added more problems for those few whites still drawn into the trade and greater dangers for the men and women who became their illegal cargoes. Slavers shifted to the sleek-lined, heavily sailed sloops and clippers of American design, which could

outsail any British patrol ship. What they gained in
speed, they gave up in space. Unwilling, however, to
lose trade, the captains packed these ships with slaves
so that, if anything, their conditions were more intoler-
able than those of the earlier slower vessels. In time,
also, many captains—enterprising Yankee skippers
often enough—rounded the Cape of Good Hope and
traded with the Arab slavers of Zanzibar and East
Africa, thereby extending the length of passage to the
New World.

All the risks to lives and capital were dependent on
the time spent at sea. The shorter the voyage, the less
likelihood disease or disaster would strike. If the trip
were merely from the Gambia River to the West Indies
under the most favorable conditions, the crossing could
be made in as little as three weeks. A longer voyage, say
from the Congo to Virginia, with trouble at sea, could
take more than three months.

Problems of raging winds and heavy seas were the
main concerns, for they could send a small craft far off
its course, wasting weeks. Or worse, the craft could be
tossed like matchwood in the towering waves, swamped
by mountainous seas, or spun off into oblivion by hurri-
cane winds. Or, the other curse of sailors, the craft
might be reduced to immobility for days on end—be-
calmed in doldrums—the sails yawning for the slightest
breeze that might pick them up again. With time lost,
troubles multiplied. Rations had to be made to stretch.
Meager at best (salt beef and hardtack for the crew;
rice, stewed yams, or plantains for slaves, and a pint of
water served twice a day), they became half-rations or
quarter-rations or less if need be. Storms brought additional problems because the hatches had to be covered;
and, as they were the only source of air to the densely

packed hold, when the hatches were reopened, many captives would have died from suffocation and would be thrown into the sea.

Those Europeans who would jeopardize their wealth and lives in the slave trade had to take all these risks into account. From one point of view, these calculations were no different from those one would make in any hazardous business venture with any other species of merchandise. Certainly, they would prefer to think so, abjuring such moral and sentimental considerations as might be raised about trading in human beings. So long as such scruples did not weaken resolve, with enterprise, daring, and luck, enormous profits were to be made from this trade. One needed merely to understand that the object of shipping was to get as much acceptable cargo to port as one could at the lowest possible cost.

Even slaves who were sick or dying, like any other damaged merchandise, could be expected to bring some price. And those who were too far gone, if detected soon enough, could be jettisoned so that they would not continue to drain food and water. That, too, was a judgment one could make with any species of cargo that proved more costly to transport than would be realized in sale or auction. All such decisions were simple enough to come by as long as one was ruthless in insisting on the analogy beween human beings and other items of commerce.

But the humanity of the Africans was a fact and could not be gainsaid by any "hard-headed" calculations. That fact made them different from all other forms of cargo, and all who trafficked in slaves had to come to know it.

Because they were human, the crew could find among the women release for their sexual hungers. That was common enough, the women being separate from the men, the voyages being long, and the women having no choice in the matter.

Because they were intelligent human beings, the captives could calculate, too, and might take their own desperate risks to break out of their oppression. They could frustrate the entire enterprise with a slave mutiny. Or individuals might take themselves out of their captors' hands by suicide. Such possibilities were constant reminders that an irreducible human quality made the forced transport and sale of Africans in the New World something different from the trade in tea and spices.

The slave trade for Europeans remained an enterprise of calculable risks. Not so for Africans. The dungeons or barracoons of the coast had been only other way stations, like the rest in the African's journey, carrying him into unknown worlds where the mind and spirit were twisted through anguish unimaginable except in fantasies of the nether world. Already the deep ruptures with self and place had occurred. One was like the dust and grasses, blown and swirled by the capricious spirits in the winds; like leaves and twigs caught up by the willful grasp of the river spirits, drawn relentlessly to the sea. Ties that had held them fast had been severed, and they were in the sway of irresistible forces. Whoever the demons possessing them, they were not done yet.

When their time came, when a ship arrived for them, the captives would be pushed into the bilge of canoes and taken through the surf to the waiting vessels. There, they would be chained in the holds. While the ship stood off the coast, the captives surely sensed the awesomeness of the moment. From the beginning there had been tales and whispers of where it was all leading, what it all meant. Whatever the horror of the tales, reality seemed to outreach fantasy. Real or imaginary, the experience did lead to this dungeon bobbing on the water.

Each place passed since the rupture had not been seen again. Until this moment, the way back, however far and difficult, was at least in the realm of the possible. But once this craft, like the coffles before, placed distance between itself and the shore, there would be no way back.

Now was the time that daring and despair would comingle so that if some saw an inattentive guard, a hatch left open, a potential weapon within reach, they might move together and sweep the ship like a hot and angry wind. It was during this time, when the ships lay off the coast, that the greatest number of slave mutinies occurred.

But even here, so close to Africa, the captives were already too ensnarled in the European system for most of these uprisings to succeed. They depended on chance: the laxness of the crew, some means to free themselves from chains, and the spontaneous agreement of the Africans that they would attack together.

But if it happened, it would be as if a spark had ignited powder: an explosion of all the hurt, rage, bewilderment, fear, and humiliation that had accumulated over miles of march and compressed over months of capture. As a holocaust, they would sweep out of the hold where they were stored, through the hatchways, onto the decks. Blacks and whites met as desperate men, for Europeans, outside their ships and enclaves of power, were isolated white flecks in a sea of blackness. Both sides, with their backs against the wall, fought viciously, as death or victory were the only possibilities. If the Africans could overcome the Europeans and their weapons, avoid being swept away by the deck guns' grapeshot, miss being swallowed by the sea under the weight of their shackles, they would take over the ship.

When the rage was spent, the practical problem remained: where to go from there? They had come into possession of a boat they could not sail. They were far from a place and circumstances where they might rely on conventional wisdom. They were already lost in another world where their experience counted for little.

First, there was the problem of making the ship go. Some mutineers forced a remnant of the crew to sail it for them. A simple bargain—life in exchange for skills. Take the ship along the coast to where it might be safe to debark. But then, the unwilling crew could be expected to try any deception to turn the tables. Others, having killed the crew, ran the ship aground, taking a chance on overland escape. Neither tactic really solved the problem. However they reached land, they would have to avoid immediate recapture.

Sailing under duress, the white crew would search every conscious moment for the sail of another ship or some sign of other white men nearby. They knew, as perhaps few Africans understood, that at the last ditch, white men of whatever nation would stand against black men. African chiefs and merchants might have been amused by the narrow and spirited competition among Europeans, who were known to cheat and even kill one another over an advantage in trade. But they were of a single mind and purpose when threatened by black men. The crew would know, therefore, that whatever the flag a ship might fly, they would find help there.

Such European solidarity was essential to the success of the slave trade. After all, the Europeans shared a sense of their tenuousness on the African coast. Always few in numbers, any concerted effort by local Africans could have pushed them into the sea. If they showed themselves weak, unable even to hold the slaves they had purchased, they might become easy victims of the capricious whims of black chiefs and merchants, whose amusement would turn to contempt. Also, they knew they had something in common, regardless of nation. For some it was racial: they were white men, the others black men; they were civilized, the others savages. For others it was religious: they were all Christians—although split by denomination—and the others were pagans. Whatever, all shared the belief that Africans were slaves and property that should not be allowed to escape through insurrection. A slave who mutined was like a desperate pirate: the treasure he sought was his person.

Not the least of the Europeans' considerations were their conventions of international trade, which made a mutinied ship a "prize," subject to the rules of salvage. This is to say, the rescuing captain, his crew, and investors might take most, if not all, of the value of the ship and its slave cargo. Such a "windfall" would seem well worth the few lives lost in capturing a mutinied ship.

However it may be explained, there was some abstraction—race, religion, opportunity—that made Europeans see themselves as having an obligation and loyalty to others of their kind; the African was alien to them all. Such racial unity was strikingly absent from the African consciousness. It was a crucial difference. If either the Europeans had lacked it or the Africans had possessed it, the forced sale and transport of blacks to the New World would never have flourished as it did.

It was precisely the absence of racial consciousness among Africans, or some other appeal to a loyalty transcending particularism and private profit, that made successful escape improbable for the mutineer. Were he to reach shore, he was most likely to fall again into the hands of Africans who would sell him for profit. And in short time, he would find himself in another ship, in irons, on his way to America. He would come to understand what Africans who were not commodities in the slave trade did not know: all white men were his enemy, and since he had an exchange value in the market, no black man could be called his friend.

His best chance to keep from being returned to chains was to become part of a mutiny that, because of tribal identity, held together against random attack until some refuge was found. Even so, it was likely to be a long, complicated, and dangerous way home—if, indeed, home still existed. Very few would ever find their way back. If a mutineer remained on or near the coast, survival—both the avoidance of recapture and the matter of living from day to day—would force him to become part of the trade in slaves. He would need to capture others, serve in the operation of merchants who could protect him, or, with power and force of will, become a merchant in the trade himself.

There were other, less violent ways that a few would use to escape the net sweeping them toward America. There needed to be luck, a certain talent, and a quality of mind that permitted one to see oneself within a system that had a logic. The system of slavery and the slave trade provoked three styles of response: resistance, adaptation, and opportunism. But opportunism required that one have not only an opportunity to grasp but the perception that there was a personal advantage to be found in the system.

The chance might fall to a young woman if she attracted the attention of an officer or agent of the sys-

tem. Be he black or white, she might be kept by him
as his concubine. Such sexual exploitation was frequent enough, but few of the women who were so used
served more than momentary needs. Some, nevertheless,
managed in this way to remain part of the growing
heterogeneous population of the trading centers. It is
impossible to say that those who stayed calculated it
so to happen, or that those who consciously tried to
insinuate themselves into the lives of the slavers often
succeeded; but for some, sex became an anchor that
would hold them against the continuing drift. And while
they were little more than slaves to the men they served,
they were able to make for themselves a place, and
from these unions would come the mulatto population
that is today scattered along the former slave coast.

Opportunity was less obvious and available to men.
Yet a man or boy, who for some reason had managed
to gather enough pieces of the European's language to
make himself understood, might also find his way into
the slaver's service. With a few words and a sense of
some African tongues, he could become a linguister,
for it was always useful to have someone capable of
explaining not only the African to the European but the
European to the captives. Seldom were such linguisters
taken from the captives. Most often they were from
coastal trading tribes. But it did happen that some escaped this way. It was a significant status because it
elevated one among others. A part of the will to serve
the system, thus, was a sense that one was no longer a
part of the mass of blacks who were herded daily
through the centers of trade. But even this elevation
within the system was tenuous at best and provided no
certain anchor against the westward drift. Black linguisters were regularly pressed into service for the
ocean crossing; and if some returned for a second voy-

age, others were set upon by hostile captives or crew in mid-passage, or sold into slavery by a deceiving captain at his last port of call.

For such people, few as there were, the system itself gave them back something they had lost. Now the mercantile enterprise was their place of belonging, offering them a limited sense of being and identity.

By far, the greatest number of captives were packed into the ships, too exhausted in body and spirit to resist or to calculate—too benumbed to hope for more than a surcease to the trial and nightmare. Hope requires a known landscape, for then one can desire the preferred way to those that lie ahead. But on the *terra incognita* where the captives were, there was no imaginable way that seemed preferable to any other. The only hope was that this was all fantasy—the whim of a malevolent spirit. Perhaps, as suddenly as it had materialized, it would be blown away, leaving one's feet planted once again on familiar earth.

The absence of hope defined only part of the void, part of a numbness of spirit. There was also the emptiness that came when fear was gone. The worst that could happen had already occurred. They had been uprooted from the world of the living and cast into space beyond meaningful death. Since nothing was real or purposeful any more, nothing was to be feared more than anything else. They had already been transported beyond the bounds of known or imagined sensibility. The shock of the first capture and the succeeding humiliation had a cumulative effect such that the next insult was no surprise and could be met with phlegmatic indifference. Yet the body did not like pain, so it might cower and shrink in anticipation of it. That came more as a reflex, a conditioned response, than as a spirited and conscious fear. So while the most horrifying tales were whispered—that they would be carried over the water until it opened and they fell into a nether world of demons, serpents, and monsters; that the white men would eat them—the spirit was too dulled for the panic of fear. For the most part, the mind and the will abdicated pretensions of supremacy, and bodily exigencies became the principal governance. Avoid pain as much as possible; when there was hunger and food, eat; when there was thirst and water, drink; when the bladder and the bowels were full, empty them; surrender mind and will to the narcotic numbness of the void.

Some captives refused or were unable to surrender. For them the realities always remained too real. Some of them through defiance, some of them through panic, would elect death for themselves rather than accept what their minds saw and their spirits felt. At every possible chance they would try to jump overboard and drown themselves in the sea. Some would refuse to eat, starving themselves to death. All slave ships were equipped for such as these. Nets were hung over the sides to catch those who would jump. Devices would be inserted between the teeth of those who refused to eat and screwed until their prongs widened, forcing the mouth to open so that food could be pushed in. Thus, the body could be made to stay alive, overruling the will to die.

The surrender of the spirit and the will to numbness was in its own way a choice of death, a retreat of the consciousness into a tomb of insensibility. Only the automatic, physiological reflexes acted on nervous response to keep the biological apparatus functioning. Sometimes the psychic shock was so great, the entombment of spirit so profound, that biological death would soon follow. Many captives simply retreated, thus, into death—from no disease and no apparently conscious

act. Europeans were baffled for an explanation. Some
claimed these captives had wanted death so badly that
they held their breath, suffocating themselves. But is
that possible? Rather, it would seem that these captives
died of shock. Almost in a void of will, the biology had
perhaps ceased functioning, and life extinguished itself
—an involuntary suicide.

Whether or not medical science had ever known such
a phenomenon, the captains of slave ships sought an
answer to it, because not only did they observe such
deaths among their human cargo, but they believed it to
have an epidemic character unless arrested. Their solution was that each day during the voyage, weather per-
mitting, the captives would be made to gather on deck
and jump up and down in what the crew called a dance.
Drums were used for rhythm; the whip was used as a
goad. It made a difference. The forced activity caused
the heart to beat faster and the blood to flow, whether
or not there was a will. Thus, it seemed, when all the
sources that fed the spirit and the mind were attenuated,
an external will had to be brought into play to sustain
life. Apparently, the rude metamorphosis of men into
commodities left little will to live. But they were forced
to live. Only then could their captors profit.

For most Africans, the sea was an unknown element,
but they would have to live on it for weeks, even
months, in the tight confines of the wind-driven boats.
Into the vast space that seemed empty—for nowhere in
the vastness was there a sign that humans belonged,
except for the vessel on which they were kept alive—
all else sank beneath the surface. Even the sea birds
that had followed from the African shore gave up the
chase after a while, and they were alone in this inhuman
domain, tossed and rocked endlessly.

Truly, it would seem an infernal voyage in a cradle

of death and oblivion. For when the mind dared to
accept its consciousness and the dim light of reality
pierced through, one would hum remembered chants.
The heart and soul would want to be propelled by the
voice through the void and darkness to familiar spirits.
Always before, in the midst of village incantation, the
sound would find its echo and amplification in other
voices, go the whole circle round, awakening the ever-
present spirits that wanted to live within. Like the
thunder following lightning, a spark of life would pass
through them all. But here, in this darkness, rocking,
the voice could awaken only the most feeble echo, and
nothing would come back on the ears save the hiss and
roar of the sea, the whine and whir of the wind, the
moans and whimperings of desolation. It was as if all
the spirits that had made life whole were deaf or dead,
or perhaps they did not inhabit the domain of the sea.

Sometimes, the eye would discern another, more familiar than the rest. The markings on his face, his look,
made him kin in that network of family, clan, and tribe
that had seemed before to be endless. He might speak
remembered words or tell of familiar places or together
they might talk of relatives, however distant. But as his
eyes opened and as one looked into them, there was the
same hollowness and emptiness that one saw all around.
Better to retreat behind one's own eyes than look into
the void of others.

Endless were the days of rocking and tossing when
the weather was at its best. But there were other times
when the whole of the craft would be tossed high in the
air and come stuttering and crashing down—twisting,
turning, spinning—while the bodies of the captives
became bloody and bruised from the rude decks. The
timbers of the ship groaned as if mocking agonized human cries: a miserable cacophony of wails and groans

and last gasps of those struggling for air in the stifling
space closed off against the storm.

Slave ships were death ships for many. And for
others, they were awful holds of filth and disease. Dysentery always took some and left the hold smeared and
smelling of blood and mucus from spasmic bowels.
Despondency of spirits and packed conditions made it
difficult to reach the few receptacles provided for excrement, so men relieved themselves where they could.
Or when one of the bound partners was too weak to
move, both had to lie in the resulting waste. Slave ships
were, thus notorious for their stench. They could be
smelled miles downwind. Other seamen preferred to
give them a wide berth.

What spark of spirit might be left in such appalling
degradation erupted in random, senseless ways, such as
in biting the legs or feet of passing sailors or the ship's
doctor. Or anger could turn against others like oneself
—especially he to whom one was bound. One might
scream and scratch and bite and claw until pulled apart,
spent and confused.

Even in abject misery there are ways of seeing grada-
tions, and the mind can find comfort, faint but real, in
a misery even deeper than one's own. Death and dying,
stumbling ineptitude, disease, and madness are in others
a mark of one's own residual strength. It could feed as
well on a sense of rivalry, personal or tribal; and clever
Europeans knew that one way to keep their captives
alive was to make survival a challenge to personal and
tribal honor.

The end of the middle passage was signaled by the
quickened life of the crew. Rations were fuller, exer-
cises were brisker, everything was done that might
enliven the spirits of the captives. After land had been

in sight, sometimes for days, the crew went over the
captives again, and the captain judged the value of his
remaining cargo. Youth against age, health against disease, strength against weakness, all was balanced out
as hands felt muscles and joints, checked eyes, gums,
and teeth. The skin was searched for signs of yaws; the
rectum was examined for signs of flux. All flaws that
were discovered would be disguised. The bodies would
be rubbed with oil to make the skin glisten, covering
over the flat tone that had resulted from the long sea
voyage. When all this was done, the captain was ready
for market. Having reached port with a live cargo,
chances are that he would have a handsome profit.
Some of the captives, however, too weak or diseased
to be sold, might be cast into the sea, at best, left to die
on the wharves. For the rest, it need merely appear that
they could be made to work and he would be able to
fetch the going market price for new Africans.

Quite often a shore-side merchant, sometimes the
captain's partner, would send among the captives a
black man, whose job it was to put them at ease and
alert the merchant to any one who might cause trouble.
To the Africans he would have a strange appearance,
wearing the European style of dress. There would be
a jauntiness, a quickness, about him—an air of assurance. He could speak to them in their languages, and he
would often know enough of where they were from to
speak of specific places and families, thus awakening
in them a sense of kinship. Some, of course, would be
kin indeed. But all was designed only to allay their fears
and prepare them for the market.

"No, the white man will not eat you; he eats too well
to need to eat you. No, there were no evil spirits at
work. All you will have to do is work, just like you have
always done. There are many, many more, you will see

them; they work hard and they eat. You need only
worry that you not be bought by a poor man, because
he will have very little and few other blacks, and you
will have to work very hard. But to be bought by a rich
man makes life better, because he feeds you better and
gives you better clothes, and there will be other blacks
to work with and be around. The secret is to look your
best, to look strong and healthy and young. That will
make many people want you and make it so only men
with much money can buy you. And don't try to run
away: there is no place to run. And don't look mean,
because only mean men will want you, and they will
make your life hard. All will go well, and you will be
glad, if you hold yourself easy."

Strange, this talk among the Africans. His voice was
reassuring and welcome. What he said had a kind of
comfort—all would be normal in time. Here were familiar sounds and cadences. One's spirit was enlivened
by the lightness and the spirit of this man. But there
was something strange and un-African about him. He
had the languages of home, and his face still bore African markings, but he was different. Perhaps it was the
way he moved so easily from one to another. Tribe mattered not; language mattered not. Even in those languages he did not know, he would try to make himself
understood. He seemed to be related to them all because he was not really related to any of them. His eyes
searched among them for signs that would profit his
master to know and thereby would profit him. This was
not kinship as the African knew it. It was something
strange and new.

The ordeal was ended. All now were in the market,
again to be estimated by eyes and hands for values that
were not quite understood. Behind the eyes of these

white men was a consciousness of a reality not shared by the captives. The white men knew and could calculate what youth and muscle would mean in terms of value produced. They had a measure of the future value of a woman, whose muscle counted as a man's but counted differently if she were in her breeding years, with children yet to attain their fullness, or if she were already beyond ripeness. Upon the shrewdness of their sense of such relative values, the futures of their own enterprises and wealth would rest. Upon such sharpness, and luck too. True evaluation of human worth is deceptive, for disease, heartache, unalterable depression, contrariness of will, could lurk beneath the most placid exterior. And those who might be bought at the highest price could prove the most troublesome in the end.

But the captives could have little sense of such calculations. Except in the roughest terms, they could have little idea why some were snatched at more eagerly than others. They were mere objects of trade, not participants in it. Up to this time—their purchase in America—they had suffered psychic and physical traumas of great magnitude. They had been cut off from everything that had given them meaning. All that had before been seen as all-powerful and all-knowing had come to seem meager and ignorant indeed. They were now captives and unfree, in alien hands. From their sale in American markets, they and their seed for two hundred years into the future were to learn the meaning of slavery, a resource by which others could pursue their own happiness.

3

Strange New World: Afro-Americanization

THE RUPTURE and the middle passage were harsh and brutal filters. The physically weak and emotionally delicate had fallen by the wayside. Survival as a whole person was not due to strength alone but came from a tenacity of will, an obstinacy, a refusal of the spirit to be engulfed by power and events.

From the first break with family to the debarkation in Maryland, Virginia, or Carolina, there had been such a reversal of roles and expectations that old patterns and standards of conduct were of dubious value. The days, months, the lifetime that lay ahead, would continue to be new—an undreamed of experience. It would require them to become new men and women—Africans, but Americans. But while this process, which had begun in the African village, would continue, much of the old would abide. It might surprise them to know what would endure of all they carried with them in their minds and hearts.

Their very first impression of America would be incorrect. They would have thought that they had arrived in the white man's country. But he, too, was a stranger in this new land. He had cut his ties with the Old World in order to make his way in America. It was a wilderness to him. He, too, would be transformed into a new man. The process—the rupture, the crossing, the settlement—would change them both, black and white, and America was to have its sway over them both. Perhaps the most affecting experience in their transformation was in adapting to each other. So, in the end, the American and American culture would be of Europe, yes, but of America, too, and far more of Africa than has been thought.

The body, the biological organism, had first to make itself at home in an unfamiliar environment. Each person, from his own place, was a cumulative product of a long selective process wherein the body refined optimal accommodation to a particular climate and food. Each person was representative of a balance that had been found between his people and the sea of life they inhabited, a delicate adaptation of organisms, from the largest and most complex to the simplest. Survival of the species had depended on well-nurtured defenses of the body against microscopic invaders, which would destroy it. These defenses were never perfect; but in the aggregate, the human species survived specific challenges in each home base.

Coming to America meant that Europeans and Africans would encounter varieties of microorganisms foreign to them and would bring with them varieties that were new to America. So with red, white, and black men merging in this place, their bodies would have to make adjustments.

Europeans had known for a long time that they were especially susceptible to fevers along the African coast.

Africans had been amused that white men were so weakened by what they called the bad air of the coasts and rivers, while black men seemed unaffected. It had been a deception, of course. Africans, too, were vulnerable to the malaria parasite and most probably carried it in an attenuated state. But they had lived with it: their bodies had become accustomed enough to the parasite to function reasonably well, building up immunities, mothers passing the defenses through the placenta to those yet to be born.

It is uncertain whether malaria existed in America before Columbus; the first known epidemic is recorded in 1493. But the black, white, and red men who were to live and work in the lowlands of the South—from Louisiana up through the Carolinas and Virginia— came to know what they were to call intermittent fevers, or fever and ague. In the swamps and marshes, wherever the anopheline mosquito could breed and put the parasite into the human blood, the disease was common.

The one-celled parasite would invade the red blood cells, splitting the pigment from the protein. After a period of incubation, when the parasite multiplied, the human host would suffer four- to ten-hour cycles of chills and fever. Normally, the symptoms would abate and the victim would live on, lethargic and in general poor health. But in severe cases there would be diarrhea, vomiting, delirium, coma, and death.

The Africans' bodies had built some defenses. Evolution in the midst of this disease gave favorable selection to the sickle-cell trait, where the red corpuscles were stunted but consequently, inhospitable to the malaria parasite. Also, the spleen, liver, and bone marrow were inclined to create macrophages, amoeba-like cells which would devour the foreign substances in the blood.

So while Africans were not immune to malaria, they were less susceptible than Europeans, and incidents of the disease were less likely to be debilitating. White colonists in America seemed to accept this difference as absolute, claiming that blacks could work better in the rice plantations of South Carolina and Georgia or the marshes and swamps of the South than could whites. During the "sickly season," whites who could took to high ground, where the air was better.

Yellow fever, also carried by a mosquito, the *Aedes aegypti*, was thought to have originated in West Africa. However, there are Mayan chronicles that describe such a disease in pre-Columbian America. After the yellow-fever virus incubated for several days, the host would experience the onset of headaches, backaches, and rapidly rising fever accompanied by nausea and vomiting. In severe cases, there would be hemorrhaging into the mucus membranes, causing the vomit to be of a dark, altered blood. Because liver cells would be destroyed by the disease, a yellowing of the skin and eyes was common, hence the malady's name. While yellow fever was often fatal, those who survived had lifetime immunity, and it would seem that the disease was less often fatal to Africans than to Europeans.

A smallpox pandemic hit Europe in the early seventeenth century, reaching England between 1666 and 1675. The Anglo-American colonies were also touched by the disease during this time. Smallpox followed a cycle of fever accompanied by skin eruptions—papules, vesicles, pustules—and scabbing. Generally, the disease left lasting pockmarks. It was an especially virulent and contagious disease. There needed to be direct contact for it to spread, but the virus could be inhaled from the clothing and effects of a victim, his living quarters, or even his corpse. A person, once immune could carry the virus and infect others.

All the peoples in America, the white and black new-comers as well as the native Indians, would have to adapt to new microorganisms as they came into the country. Indians were especially vulnerable to small-pox, and it did much to reduce their population. Afri-cans also might well have been at a disadvantage to Europeans, and it became common to consider a slave more valuable if he had the scars of the pox, indicating his immunity. On the other hand, blacks tended to ac-commodate better than whites to malaria and yellow fever, but they were particularly susceptible to respira-tory infections and pneumonia. Asian cholera was new to them all. It entered the country in 1832 through Canada and traveled down the Mississippi Valley, spreading east and west, hitting New York and Boston especially hard. There was no prior experience of it and no treatment. Each person alike had to meet the disease for the first time.

Still Africans in the semi-tropical South could rely on their folk medicines and their herbs in a way that Europeans could not. When they were ill, each would call upon what knowledge, what "science," was theirs to meet the problems. Thus, African lore about herbs and medicines was to survive long after its source would be forgotten.

Curiously, when Cotton Mather, the New England divine and scientist, entered a debate urging the intro-duction of inoculation techniques in Massachusetts in 1721, he called upon the experience of Africans to bolster his case. They had reported that in the old country, many had died from smallpox until the prac-tice was begun of cutting the skin of those not affected and placing in the wound the secretion from the pox. The Africans claimed it would make them mildly ill, but they would not die nor would they catch the pox again. Thus converged the "science" of Europe and Africa.

Afro-Americanization began in the first forced contacts with strangers—other blacks of peculiar aspect and habit, white men from beyond the seas. It began in the frantic and hysterical efforts to explain oneself, to say who one was, where one belonged, to plead to be returned—all to men who seemed not to hear. Nothing more immediately showed the world to be upside down than that one's words bounced back, unattended, and those of others seemed a cacophony, a gibberish. At its worst, meaning was reduced to gestures of hands, arms, and head, to grunts and explosive sounds, and to physical force.

Except for those so shocked as to be dumb to all meaning, a human will to communicate would span the chasm. The ears detected familiar sounds, perhaps strange inflections, among Africans from other parts, and minds stretched to understand and be understood. The process of Afro-Americanization obliterated, in due course, age-old barriers that had existed among Africans. Bridges of language were the first efforts to link them into one people.

Communication was also necessary as a tool of trade. European traders and their African partners had to find words and signs—a code—which would allow their business with one another to advance with minimal misunderstanding. So language on both sides—African and European—reduced itself to bare simplicity, free of subtleties and complexities. There developed languages of European and African vocabulary and simplified syntax. Such blends, based on African with Portuguese, French, and English, became the *linguae francae* of the Atlantic basin.

The pidgin languages that served the traders also allowed the captives to understand and be understood. The slave traders, and later the slave owners, preferred to mix the Africans, avoiding concentrating any one people together. This strategy rested on the desire to play on traditional hostilities and language differences so as to prevent conspiracies and uprisings. Yet, this mixture of tongues itself encouraged the invention of new languages. African languages within language families were not so dissimilar that those who would put forth effort could not be understood. Out of the mix and flux of people, various pidgins were born.

Children, despite the shock of rupture, found it easy to mouth new sounds for old meanings. Adults, on the other hand, would know how a thing was supposed to be said, and they would never feel new words approximated what they meant to say. They would always be uneasy that they were not being understood or that they had missed something said to them.

White men who wanted Africans to labor had to understand them and be understood. It might appear to the slave buyer, as he picked among newly arrived Africans, that they talked a "gibberish," and he might hope to have someone familiar with African languages to communicate for him. But his success as a master of African slaves would depend on his sharing a common language. He had to learn and contribute further to a workable pidgin dialect.

Circumstances and personality determined how the African fared. For some, the heart had been forever closed by tragedy, and the mind and spirit would never open to accept the new reality; the tongue would never untie itself in crude and alien sounds. Most, living among others like themselves, used the convenience of language to draw them together. There were a few whose company was mainly whites, whose language picked up more of the cadences and sounds of Ireland or England. Others would find themselves among Indians, learning and teaching words. Occasionally, there would be one like Phyllis Wheatley, brought from Africa at the age of nine, petted in a New England household, educated on the standard Greek and Latin classics, who would write poetry in the language of Alexander Pope. She was to be the second American woman after Anne Bradstreet, to publish a book of poems in the English language.

Most African immigrants were to find their lives among others like themselves, with few whites about. Since they spoke most often to one another, there was little need to measure their words against an English spoken by whites. As generations passed and children native to America grew up, their language was to be an expansion and development of that used on the plantations. It would be their native tongue—thought in and spoken in as a natural thing—not artificial and strained as it had been with their mothers and fathers. It was familiar to them, just as it would have become familiar to whites with whom they spoke. Thus, their masters, now also a native American generation, could describe them as "country born" and speaking a "good" or "sensible" English, even though it was no less the language of black men and women on plantations.

English settlers made little effort to teach Africans English and made none to learn African languages; but each people had to find a halfway point. As they both became more skillful at it, the whites would come to consider the blacks more "sensible."

White men and women also became more "sensible"
as time went on. Their tongues became accustomed to
"goober," "tote," "gumbo," "banjo," "cooter," "chig-
ger," "yam," "okra," "juke," and other such words
from Africa. They picked up word patterns and tonali-
ties as well. Through the generations following the first
"country born" of both races, black and white children
grew up together, playing the same games, using the
same words. It would take a sensitive ear to distinguish
native white from native black language. Many foreign
visitors who came to the South in the nineteenth century remarked that English in the South had much to do
with black influence.

Africa persisted in the language in subtle ways. Africans had often named their children according to the
days of the week. There were day names for both boys
and girls. Quashee or Quasheba, Cudjo or Juba, Cuba,
Abba, Cuffee or Phibbi, all were to echo through two
centuries, although sometimes in distorted form. English ears heard these sounds differently. So they were
to be written in the plantation journals as Squash or
Sheba, Joe, Abby, Cuff or Phoebe. White men might
think that Juba was a dance and not Monday, that Cuba
was an island and not Wednesday. They might think of
the name Jack when they heard the name Quack. They
might smile at what they heard as poor elocution, changing the name to sound right to their own ears. But black
mothers and fathers continued to understand that the
name stood for a given day or a season. In time, as
Africa and England blended into America, black children would be given names like Monday, Friday, or
Saturday, Winter or Summer.

Down into the nineteenth century, African names
would survive. Ledgers of the slave merchant Dr. Louis
de Saussure, dated 1864, list slaves named Rinah, Sum-

mer, Saturday, Kezia, Molsey, Sopha, Cinda, Tyra, Winter, Nelpey, and Sukey. Some were Anglicized versions of what had once been African; others were pure continuations of African names.

Language is a way of bringing people together, and it did bring diverse African words into the English-, French-, or Spanish-based Creoles. But language is also a way of maintaining social distance among people, and it did that too in the new American tongues. Europeans and Africans had always made distinctions among themselves by how one used words. The higher orders marked themselves off from the lower by accent, tone, diction, and vocabulary. So, too, in America, Negro speech and white speech became marks of social disparity. Those blacks who mastered the white man's language were, in so doing, placing themselves socially at a remove from those blacks who did not. How a black person would come to speak American English would depend on more than opportunity, intelligence, and facility. There needed to be a choice to emulate white people, the ability to slip from one style of speech into another when the occasion warranted, and the willingness to bear the ridicule of fellow blacks who might think him a mimic and sycophant.

White people, however, were anxious to keep their language to themselves. They wanted it as an emblem of the social superiority they felt to blacks and the lower orders. They wanted to talk to one another, among blacks, and not have their meaning understood. They wanted language to serve in limited ways to communicate between themselves and slaves, but they also wanted it to remain enigmatic. Language to them was a mark of civilization as well as a tool of communication, and they needed the sense of security a monopoly on good speech and literacy gave them. Furthermore, they knew that language transported ideas, and ideas could be weapons against established order. So, rather than finding a prideful, missionizing achievement in the acculturation of Afro-Americans into English, the Anglo-Americans were protective and jealous. Above all, as far as it was possible, slaves were to be kept ignorant of the written word.

Blacks, too, had their secret codes, the most obvious and universal being drum sounds. Significantly, the earliest slave laws made the use of drums a criminal act for slaves. The need for secrecy would encourage blacks to hold on to African elements as long as they could. They also worked to speak in symbol, parable, and metaphor. They masked meaning by stories and song. White prohibitions against reading gave an almost cabalistic weight to the written word (the Bible); there was something magical in translating marks on a page into meaning, in making the book "talk." Some learned to read as an underground thing, secret and forbidden.

Like all oppressed people, black Americans learned that in talking to whites, language could be a shield. Whites presumed that blacks knew little, and whites often showed the strain in trying to make themselves understood. It was easy enough to hide behind the barrier of language, to feign ignorance or incomprehension. To fall suddenly dumb before the white master's words was an instinctive evasion, a first line of defense.

An American language and style emerged out of the blendings of peoples—European, African, and Indian. Not merely did new words come into English, but cadences, rhythms, and inflections were affected. Characteristic ways the body moved in gesturing, the head was held, the eyes were cast, were formed from a relationship where two language codes were assumed, where one people was presumed servile and deferential, the other authoritative and masterful.

Aside from the human interaction, America itself called for invention, for expression beyond conventional language. The frontier wilderness, the rawness of the coupling of people and nature, the collisions of people with one another outside legal and social systems of control, the unspeakable grandeur of the country, all called forth a lexicon befitting the experience. When white men and black men exploded onto the frontiers or into the riverboats and barges of the Ohio and Mississsippi, they wanted to blow themselves up to the size of the country. The stories they told became incredible, challenging a reality that itself was beyond belief. And their words grew with strange inventions: absquatulate, slantendicular, cahoot, catawampus, spyficated, flabbergasted, tarnacious, bodacious, rampagious, concussence, supernatiousness, rumsquattle. Genteel Easterners would call such language gibberish and their inventors savages, but it was merely that America and Europe and Africa were building a language to fit the country.

Africans had preconceptions about how the universe was ordered, how each was linked with other beings and things, both in the time that was past as well as in the time that was yet to come. The African knew himself to be one with nature; everything about him was, like himself, a being in nature. Animals, plants, and trees had spirit and life within them—even stones, houses, and rivers had indwelling spirits. The force of creation had caused them all—was in them all—and those who had passed beyond the living left a spirit that abided. The African's world was intermixed with tangible and spiritual realities, which wove him into all of nature, and the present into all pasts and all futures.

This was the world in which the African had found his meaning. He would rediscover himself in America as he adapted his world view to the institutions and practices he encountered. In time, most Africans would become some variety of Christian. But this European religion would be the shell their faith was to inhabit, and they would alter that religion as their spirit moved through it. There would remain an African texture and tone to black Christianity, and some would say that the white American's religious imagination would never totally free itself of the touch of Africa.

It was easy for those Africans who settled in French and Spanish colonies to find themselves within Catholicism. The Catholic church in Europe obliged its colonial priests to bring Africans and Indians into the church. But more important, the religions of Catholics and Africans were already close in many ways. Both were ceremonial and ritualistic. The Catholic liturgy was rich with music and incantation. Africans had habitually called upon the spirits of past great ones; Catholics prayed that saints would intercede for them with God. And those saints, Jesus, and Mary were physically represented with icons, incorporating the spirit when properly blessed. The body and the blood of Christ were more than symbolically present in the host and wine of communion. Tokens of saints were worn as amulets to protect the wearer against evil. It was assumed that "relics," threads from garments or pieces of bone attributed to saints had special powers. Catholicism, like African religions, was a rich world of magic and mystery.

The Africans imagination moved freely into such a world. They had never felt themselves to have a monopoly on gods. They were always open to new ones, especially when they seemed to have power, as was apparent with the European one. But the inclusion of new names for dieties and a new way of speaking old things did not mean the abandonment of the old. Blacks could sing Catholic chants, pray to Catholic saints, and feel the genuine power of the spirit moving through ritual and ceremony. But it would be hard to separate the old from the new.

Even so, Africa was not to be restrained in the bounds of European formalism. Although officials forbade what they called paganism, blacks found secret places to worship their own gods. Voodoo or Vodûn, as was the common name, was celebrated in near-African rites, with priests and priestesses, possessed dancers, and animal sacrifice. In this nexus, spells and charms were spun and let loose, so that the slightest change in one's life—good or bad fortune, happy or unhappy love, good or ill health—could be traced to men and women who had the power to conjure. Thus, Africa lived in the way these black men and women confronted life and explained its mysteries outside the formal church more than within. Is it strange that the power of this vision, captured in all the informal parts of life, reiterated in tales and folklore, would capture the white imagination too? When loves and life and death confronted them with mystery, they were known furtively to glance toward voodoo for answers and cures.

The Puritanism of the New England settlers was at the farthest spiritual remove from Catholicism. An extreme of the Reformation, Puritanism had moved to New England in protest against the "Roman" character of the Anglican church. It would reduce religion to man and God in naked encounter, without the trappings of elaborate ceremony. Religious service was a lecture, an explication and evocation. Music and festivals were practically eliminated. Praying to icons and figures representing anyone or anything was, to them, sinful idolatry. There was only one intermediary between a person and God, and even Christ was dwarfed beneath the awesomeness of the Creator.

But beyond the austerity of its religious service, the Puritan imagination included a rich lore. This imaginative world knew of preternatural powers. God, indeed, acted in the world for his own mysterious ends. But Satan, too, invaded the world and people's lives, tempting and corrupting them. While the "laws" of nature could not be understood by people, there was nothing immutable to God's will. So, while there might be a natural explanation for events, those same events might also signal the workings of forces beyond the human ken. The smallest occurrence might have hidden meanings. An epidemic that might fell many in the towns, an unexpected dry spell or unusual rains, a cow gone suddenly dry, all might be subject to endless analysis and speculation. For God worked in mysterious ways, his wonders to unfold; and the Devil, too, often held sway. It was known that the Devil would take over creatures and humans, possess them, for his evil purposes.

It was not strange, then, that the divines and men of science would assume that the strange events of Salem, Massachusetts, in 1692 should be the work of the Devil taking over the bodies of people. Neither is it surprising that a slave woman, Tituba, would be the central witness corroborating the story of the witches. The disorders, in fact, seem to have been provoked by tales that she told to young girls. Tituba, a black woman from Barbados, and the judges and scholars of the colony, shared the same imaginary worlds and found similar explanations for events in the physical world.

In the colonial period, Protestants were nowhere open or welcoming of Africans into their fellowship; nor were the New England congregations, where conversion and membership implied a voice in church affairs, nor the Southern churches, where the enslavement of Christians was at first disconcerting. Northern blacks were made to conform like others to the strictures of a well-ordered Christian community, rarely actually being accepted as members of the congregations. In the South, despite efforts of Anglican church officers to encourage the conversion of Africans, slave owners demurred. Aside from the moral problem, they suspected Christian doctrine would be subversive to a well-ordered slave society.

The first generation of Africans were, therefore, for the most part, free of systematic Christian religious education. But everywhere slaveholders suppressed pure African practices, so their worship varied widely. All depended on circumstance and opportunity. Where blacks were thinly dispersed in the white population, conformity was easy. But on plantations, where white contact was slight, worship held close to remembered ways. Christianity made slight inroads where masters were reluctant or indifferent and where the potential black convert faced pressure and ridicule from his fellows.

The Great Awakening of the eighteenth and nineteenth centuries opened American Protestantism to the Afro-American. Evangelists preached a gospel that put spirit and heart over mind. They undermined the didacticism of the American church, shifting the emphasis from human impotence to human possibility for redemption. A person needed only to open his heart to the Holy Spirit to be saved—make himself the receptacle of divine will. This evangelical movement tended to break through the formalisms of church, opening religious experience to people through an exhorting preacher. The Great Awakening was the beginning of an American revivalist tradition, which was to sweep the countryside in spasmodic waves, drawing in blacks and being changed by that fact.

The Methodist and Baptist denominations most affected this gospel. In their relatively loose and democratic structures, and in their unashamed acceptance of spirit and emotionalism, they were the most hospitable to Afro-Americans.

The white congregants, however, were seldom pleased with black membership in their churches. While admitted to the churches, blacks were generally segregated to pews in the rear or the balcony and sometimes were obliged to hold separate services. It was these restrictions as well as the constraints they felt in white congregations that inspired the formation of the first Afro-American churches: Silver Bluff, South Carolina, in 1773, Boston in 1808, and Philadelphia in 1816.

Worshiping separately, even as Christians, allowed the African tradition to linger and survive through the black preacher, who was more exhorter than pastor. His language and style was filled with cosmic imagery, punctuated rhythmically by sounds like drums rather than words—grunts and claps of hands—one voice in a chorus of voices of the congregants. The worship was not the message of one man to his flock. Rather, it was the birthing, expanding, sustaining of an atmosphere in which all worshipers were transported. It rose and intensified with the preacher's words against the hums and responses of the congregation, until the spirit was palpable in their midst. The Holy Spirit moved among them and through them, possessed them, until one or another's body moved; sounds came from their mouths

as if another's will were within them, making their
bodies move in spasms and jerks, shaping the sounds of
their shouts.

Worship was the evoking of religious experience
through the collective, rather than the individual, will.
This was common in black religious practice, more subdued perhaps in Northern and urban churches, more
full and spontaneous in the plantation cabin or woods
—but Africa survived in them all.

Christianity was informed in subtle ways by the
legacy of Africa and the slave experience. The fine,
doctrinal issues that made all the difference between
Protestant sects and denominations were of little consequence to black men and women. The African mind
had always conceived a unity between the ultimate creative power, spirit, and the being of the first fathers;
there need be no such rationalization as the Trinity to
explain the obvious. Perhaps adult baptism made the
Baptist denomination more appealing to Southern
blacks, who enjoyed the collective ritual and for whom
it might have awakened dim recollections of water rites
in the old country. But to the black mind, Christianity
was a unity more likely to be divided between white
practices and black practices than between denominations.

Afro-American Christianity was less guilt-burdened
than white Christianity. Evil and sin existed, but they
were forces of the universe, not of man's natural condition. The Devil played his role in the world, but he resembled the trickster of African lore—like the joker in
a deck of cards, changing all the rules on whim. Man
could be the victim of Satan, but the repentant man
could find his excuse in the Devil, not in himself. Man
was weak but not corrupt. The Africans transformed
their sense of cosmic life force into the term "God,"

and in that way they never quite lost the idea that everything was subsumed under it, even man. So, God was responsible for man's weakness, and in his ultimate wisdom understood man's frailties. The wayward person could know, therefore, that he was never really lost, so long as he could open himself to the power of life that would unfold within him.

Afro-American Christianity never lost its fundamentally collective and social character. In this, it differed quite markedly from most forms of American Christianity. The highly individualistic thrust of Puritanism characterized early American Protestantism and was modified but not changed by the introduction of revivals. The typical black Christian, however, understood all religious experience to be generated by the community at worship; the congregation and the meeting were all important.

Europeans used the word "Lord" to refer to the son of God, but the word has associations with feudal and magisterial authority. Black Christians called Jesus "Lord," of course, but the word also symbolically touched on the lamb of God, the Spirit, themselves, and all godly manifestations. The prayers of black Christians were less likely to be supplications upward to authority than they were to be directed both outward and inward to establish the unity of spirit with self, to be one in the body of God.

The most fervent and common prayer was "Come Jesus, come Lord. Be among us now." The ultimate of the religious service and the religious experience was the felt unity of self with community and with the divine. Worship, when it succeeded, provided that unity in this world rather than in otherworldly dreams. Heaven and the mansions of the Lord were nevertheless constant visions of the black Christian; and while he might talk of damnation and Hell, it played less central a part in his life than it did for whites. Black Christians talked as intimates with the Lord and Biblical characters— Brother Moses, Sister Mary, Brother Jonah. To become Christian meant to join that extended family.

Black Christians dwelt more in the Old Testament than the New, not merely because, as slaves, they identified with the Hebrew children, but because those books conformed more to their own instincts for tribal and clan dieties. They resonated, as well, with the oral tradition to which Afro-Americans were attuned. In the New Testament, while their masters would find comfort and support in Paul, black Christians doted on the Jesus story, the parables, and the Crucifixion,

Such religion was intimate and personal, yet inclusive and familial. It was not of the head, rationalizing an authority for owning and exploiting fellow creatures. It was of the heart, which opened itself to feeling and affirmed one's place in the order of all creation.

The African immigrant to America, whether or not he became Christian, placed himself within a natural order that was of him but beyond him too. He had lived in intimate contact with nature, never far removed from the influence of the flux and pulse of the universe. All around him were objects—not of man's design or creation—with which man must live on intimate and peaceful terms. Man, and all that was around him, was commonly tied to the rhythms of life. All things of nature, even stones, were animated by spirit and personality. Domestic animals, and even wild beasts, were known to have distinctive characters.

Man, therefore, could never hold too exalted a place in this world of nature. His existence depended on his sympathy with the balances of which he was part.

Adapting himself to that nature, he could and should manage and cultivate it. But he must always be careful to propitiate the spirits, lest he suffer for bruising the land, uprooting trees, or dislodging stones. He could never presume to be master.

The same might be said of any peasant people who came to North America. But the African immigrants and their progeny were destined to remain, through slavery, a peasant people during much of their history. They never abandoned this view of man's oneness with nature, not only because their lives remained intimate with the throb of nature but because, deprived of much other support, this view continued to sustain them as meaningful in the universe. Whether they were to become Christians, hold to fragments of African practice, or abandon formal ritual, this pantheism would pervade the Afro-American spirit. As they looked upon white men who, more and more, would presume to be not only masters of other men but of their own world and their destiny, blacks could not help but feel a sense of their own moral superiority.

It was the intangibles—the things of the mind and spirit—that survived best: what could not be grasped by the hand and thrown away; what could not wear out, impossible to find again; those things that could lose themselves in ubiquity. It was so with African music, the way the song was voiced, the way the body moved in dance.

Music was spirit, manifest in tone and rhythms. It survived the middle passage and passing generations as if it were the soul of the people. It had its special way. The music moved with rhythms set against one another —merging and diverging—shrill tones of quills or flutes

weaving within, chasing rhythm, voices marking cadences. Most often, it was ensemble music, made to
engulf everyone and everything.

Almost every African event occurred within its own
music—religious ceremonies and rites, alike. But everything was a religious ceremony: initiations, marriages,
healing, planting, harvesting, battles, funerals. History
itself, the grandeur of the people, their heroes and
chiefs, were recalled in song. For the African coming to
America, it must have seemed that suddenly life had
been flattened out, as if the eye saw a narrower range
of colors, the ear heard only muted tones. For it was a
world where normal and extraordinary events passed
without the sound of drums, without music and the
celebration of dance.

But Africans had buried in their heads and hearts
what that music was and how to make it. They impro-
vised their instruments. Percussion had always had a
central part, and drums were made by stretching sheep-
skins over eel pots or hollow logs; sticks and bones
served as well, anything that could be struck rhythmically with fingers, hands, or feet. Reeds were cut to
various lengths to make the whistlelike quills, sticks
hollowed out for the flutes. Horsehair was stretched
over gourds to make what were called banjars. And the
body made music too: hands clapping against hands
and thighs, feet pounding against the earth, clothing
and ornaments swishing and ringing as the body jumped
and turned. Without forethought, music had been
squeezed into the baggage the Africans brought with
them, and it would prove to be their most precious possession.

Traditional music was easier to reproduce on the
islands of the West Indies, where Africans were left
more to themselves in larger numbers and where the

drum was not to be forbidden as it would be on the continent. But even in Virginia, the Carolinas, and New Amsterdam, the banjo, tambourine, flute and quill emerged. And the voices would echo ancient ways—striking the European ear as odd—with gutteral cries and moans, falsetto breaks, and antiphony.

Work would find its own music. Rhythms marked the tasks of the field, the carrying of goods onto riverboats and barges, the shucking of corn. Each task had its special rhythm and compelled its own work song: rowing on the river, clearing off the land, planting seed, hoeing and chopping. Such songs would be done in unison with a single voice to phrase each new line, the chorus to respond in refrain—for hours it would continue, pacing, commanding body movements, relieving monotony. As it had been at home, it would be again in this strange new world.

With the music, the body moved; music and dance were one. The song and rhythm paced the body in its work; the body in its dance made music. All was a unity. All were performers; all were audience. Even as one man contrived the fast and intricate steps of the juba, all others in their voices, hands, and feet were his accompaniment. Even as one woman shuffled the insinuating calinda against a man's athletic and inventive steps, all others made the music, changing off with the central dancers in the seemingly endless dance.

The African dance was to be subdued on the American continent. Nevertheless, in those places where it could, it exploded in festivals of European origin. In colonial New York, Pentecost became the occasion for the Africanized Pinkster festival with dancing, drumming, and the elevation of an African "king." Market day in Manhattan would be climaxed by dance competitions among blacks. New Orleans became the center of Africanized music and dance in such festivals as Mardi Gras. And following the revolution on Saint-Dominique, newly imported West Indian blacks made Congo Square in New Orleans the center of African music and dance it was to remain far into the nineteenth century. Other places that were isolated from the flux of American life—the Sea Islands of Carolina and Georgia—would hold most firmly to African forms in music and dance. But it all was a muted and subdued expression of Africa.

The rare, joyous moments that slavery permitted would be remembered as accompanied by music and dance. Songs came with special events like corn shucking or quilting. But often after harvest and almost always at Christmas, there would be days of dances when slaves would visit neighboring plantations. The music was supplied by fiddle, banjo, bones, or tambourine. The dancers would perform the juba or the shuffle or the double shuffle. The women moved their feet in a small heel-and-toe shuffle while their hips, bodies, and arms gyrated in what Europeans called a lascivious manner. The men moved around them, bodies provocative, eyes suggestive.

The names of their dances often claimed an identity with nature and animal life. There was the chicken wing, the buzzard lope, and snake hips. While these were all solo dances, individual men and women would exchange with one another, showing agility and inventiveness. This relationship of group and virtuoso performance marks all Afro-American music, into its manifestation in jazz.

In time, European formal dances—reels, quadrilles, and cotillions—were to take over in the slave cabins. The black musicians became adept at playing and calling these dances—for whites as well as for blacks. But no observer was unaware of the differences in the way blacks interpreted these dances and their music—the freedom with which they moved their hips, shoulders, and arms; the precision with which they marked the rhythms. They would be dancing to reels, schottisches, and polkas, but their bodies would push the forms to limits before unknown. Afro-Americans did to conventional European dance what they would to Methodist hymns. They adapted them, but in the process converted them into something that was uniquely their own and American.

To the African mind, there was no sharp distinction between the sacred and the profane. Surely, the music and dance occasioned by an initiation or a funeral was different from the satirical songs invented for ridicule. But the sacred was expressed in music and dance. Protestants in America drew a sharp line between that which men did for God—most often solemn and austere—and what they did for pleasure—always suspect of evil. It was especially so with a music that was exuberant and pushed people beyond good order, and with a dance that compelled the body to move to its own rhythm—vital, insinuating, carnal. White Americans were quick to express their shock at what they heard and saw to be the wildness of Africans.

Black Americans who became Christians were also to say that something called dance was evil. Strange, because they continued to worship in a way that perceived music and body movement as the outward manifestation of the living spirit. In their ring shouts, they moved in a circle to chanting and to the rhythmic beat of hands, their feet did the familiar heel-toe shuffle, and they would move with quickened tempo until the spirit exploded within and possession carried them away. But that was not dancing, they would say. In dancing you crossed your feet, you raised your hands high.

In the old country, they would not have had to draw such neat lines because all things merged, one into the other. Everything partook of the sacred. But in Protestant America, everything was divided between good and evil, black and white. The Afro-Americans worshiped through their bodies moving to music just as their forebears had. The most devoted black Protestant would continue so, even as he relegated dance to the profane.

The African origins in music resonate through the Afro-American experience into our own time. Its antiphonies and rhythms would remain in rhetoric, music, and dance. Afro-Americans, in time, were to take up European forms—marches, waltzes, ballads, and the belle canto opera—and their magic would convert it all into a new music. Africans came thus to be creative instruments in American culture. Eventually Euro-Americans would be willing to point to a distinctive Afro-American music and dance as essentially American. But, more to the point, they would be unable to say that their music and dance was not of Africa too.

They had been many different peoples when they were brought to America. They had been rice farmers, yam growers, herders and drovers, and river-dwelling peoples. They had worshiped Islam or the numerous special dieties that had sustained their people through time. They had been deep black in color, but also there had been many with red and yellow tones. They had had in common only the special immigration experience of being captive and slave.

Some of what they had experienced was shared by all

who came or were to come from an Old World framework to the New World. The Americanizing experience
began with the rupture from the network of traditional
relationships, cushioned by time and lore, homogeneous, organic, and resistant to change. It involved the
re-establishment and rediscovery of the self in a new
context: thin in culture and history, tenuous in tradition, heterogeneous, radically dynamic. In these affects,
the Angolan immigrant differed little from the East
Anglian.

Beyond the experience of coming, America itself,
the physical fact of it—the wilderness, the newness, the
need for invention, the jumble of peoples—imposed its
own demands and exerted its own price on all who
arrived. While Europeans might have fancied that they
were re-creating what had been familiar—New Nether-
lands, New Sweden, New England—they managed to
keep intact little beyond the external structure. While
Africans would be unable to preserve rituals, customs,
or language in forms that would be immediately recog-
nizable in their old world, they transplanted Africa to
America in such a way that the emerging culture would
be of them as they were of it. It was not that Europeans
preserved badly or well, or that Africans acculturated
to Europeans in part or in full. Rather, it was that European and African immigrants, through their experiences
together, created an American culture and an American
character.

If one had stood on a wharf in Charleston in the
eighteenth century, one would have been struck by the
differences among black people. Any prospective slave
buyer would know that there were many kinds of Africans, and he would think himself wise in believing that
he knew their different characteristics. By the mid-nineteenth century, however, almost all distinctions had

vanished. Tribal markings almost ceased to be seen. Except for the Sea Island Gullah and the Louisiana Creole, these people had come to speak a common language. Their African heritage had lost its fineness and distinctiveness, merging into a general culture to which all Afro-Americans could sense they belonged. In this instance, if in no other, the American experience was to make one people out of many.

Yet in one crucial way, the Africans' immigration experience differed from that of others. Europeans, generally on some level, had made the choice to come. Africans had not. Presumably, Europeans calculated their alternatives—doubtless, sometimes narrow and unappealing—and chose to go to America. All of them would rationalize their decision in terms of chance, the opportunity that was to be had in the New World. It was a new land, open to exploitation, promising a new life. Africans could have no such vision, because when Europeans forced their migration, it was only in the expectation that Africans would become a part of what was to be exploited. They would be instruments of others' opportunity.

To the Euro-American imagination, America continued to be an almost endless resource for opportunity, wealth, and improvement of fortune. The Afro-American might be part of that resource but not a beneficiary of it. When white Americans chose to break their political ties with Europe, searching for a language that would capsulate the validity of their experience, they spoke of the inalienable rights to life and liberty. Then they Americanized the European Enlightenment formula, changing the word "property" (static and objective) to the phrase "pursuit of happiness" (subjective, acquisitive, exploitative). The change was emblematic of what America and Americanization would mean to

Europeans right into modern times. From the beginning, it was never imagined that America should mean opportunity and the pursuit of happiness to Africans and their progeny. So while they would become Americans like the others—in some ways, more than others—that exclusion from "the dream" would make all of the difference in the world.

4

The Changing Context

THE SLAVERY of Afro-Americans had been a crucial element in American history from 1619 until the ultimate convulsion of nation making in the Civil War. There was no region or social sector unaffected or untouched. All would be included: those who from the beginning saw black men and women and their children as a means to building their own fortunes; those like the merchants of New England who were uneasy about an exotic people in their midst but nevertheless happy to profit from the trade in slaves; those who fled from competition with unfree labor, nurturing bitterness as they went and a phobia of blacks whose slavery demeaned free labor; and those whose moral senses were revolted by the idea that humans could own other humans like cattle. All who were to be Americans, including European, African, and Asian peoples yet to enter the vortex, would be touched by the fact of slavery, even generations after slavery's end. But it would be the Afro-American who would know this truth most of all—North or South, slave or free—for generations into our own time.

Making Africans into slaves in the American colonies was not a difficult decision, nor was it such a worrisome question as to cause thoughtful men to debate the matter and explore its consequences. Certainly, in the Southern colonies, men made their choices and designed appropriate legal apparatus with a reckless casualness, given the consequences that were to follow.

It was never, to them, a question of whether labor should be free or unfree, whether the poor and unpropertied should be indulged with humanitarian considerations or not. They were men of a society that regarded servants and laborers as base people, for whom hunger and the lash could be the only goad to productivity. They were accustomed to a system of labor in which these persons served long terms under a master's authority without what we would call liberty. Ordinary offenses against order were as a matter of course followed by corporal punishment—the lash, maiming, dismemberment. Offenses against property, life, and public safety were answered with capital punishment, often of an awful brutality—torture, the rack, beheading, burning at the stake, impaling.

It required, therefore, no leap of imagination, no reordering of mind or values, to introduce Africans into the society as exploitable labor without liberty, to serve the will of a master on the pain of cruel suffering or death. This is not to say that the weight of class and servility did not fall more lightly on white laborers than black, for blacks undoubtedly suffered more. But in this respect the differences were more in degree than in kind. Nothing was to prevent the full weight of oppression from falling on any given white man or woman, as it routinely did on blacks.

The crucial difference came in the acceptance of blacks exclusively as a labor source, the principal labor source, making them bound to their masters for life as would be their children, who would follow the condition of the mother. In this way, even the seed of white men —even of the master class—would be captured in the net of slavery. The custom was established not by one carefully thought out decision but over time, through refinements designed to correct apparent "faults" in the system. Thus the loophole where the black man's seed escaped slavery through the womb of a white woman was closed by, first, making such a white woman and her children serve the black man's master, and then by punishments for miscegenation so severe as to make sex between black men and white women an uncommon occurrence.

There had been confusion in attitudes regarding slavery during the first years in Virginia. Many of the slaves had come from the West Indies, were English speaking and open to religious conversion. Some of them were freed in time because masters had assumed that like other unfree servants, they were due their liberty after a term of service. Some masters had assumed it illegal to hold fellow Christians as slaves, so with proof of conversion, they felt compelled to set such people free. But in practice, even before laws made it official, Virginian planters began to treat blacks as lifetime investments. This change in attitude reflected a growing sense that colonial enterprise would depend on black labor. The laws followed as a stamp of consensus among that class of men able to exploit this form of labor. Whatever the assumptions in 1620, by 1700 Virginia was committed to the importation of Africans as an exclusive labor class.

The white Virginians may have thought pushing standard servant conditions to the limits of possibility a logical step necessary with an exotic people. Doubtless, some of the master class in Virginia and England would have seen slavery as a fit condition for the English poor, the Irish, and the Scots. While there was some talk of it, something—perhaps the fear of public outrage or the weight of tradition against it—stopped them from taking that next step with Europeans. But Africans had no advocates able to stir wide public revulsion in England, nor did they have any presumption of traditional status in English society. It would be a century before Englishmen would be sufficiently moved to end the slave trade.

Other Southern colonies would, in time, adopt the patterns of Maryland and Virginia. South Carolina settlers came with the clear intent of following the example of West Indians as much as Virginians, resting their settlement on an imported black labor force. Georgia settlers at first were inhibited from importing slaves by the philanthropic intent of the colony, but they successfully overcame what they saw to be a competitive disadvantage. If that colony was to thrive, it would have to rely on more than redeemed convicts and social misfits.

New England, however, was not hospitable to African slavery. It was not the region's soil or the climate that made slavery unattractive, although Africans probably did have more difficulty adapting to colder climates: they were especially susceptible to pulmonary and respiratory disorders. Still, Africans, in small numbers, were brought into New England, and they survived very well. The Dutch in New Amsterdam had made good use of African labor and, far from being concerned about their frailty and inefficiency, only complained that there were not enough of them. In any event, the mortality of Africans was never a deterrent to slavery where there was sufficient economic reward to compensate for the loss in capital.

It is true that New Englanders did not go in for the plantation-style of agriculture, which seemed best to exploit slave labor. But, just as Southerners, they could have made slavery work if they had wanted to. Large-scale agriculture was certainly a possibility, and the soil did not seriously limit crops. Tobacco, which supported Virginia's and Maryland's slave systems, grows on large farming operations in the Connecticut Valley in the twentieth century. Why not three centuries ago? Of course, plantation agriculture did not exhaust the possible uses of a labor bound for life, hereditary to a capitalist entrepreneur. The way could have been found had there been the will.

New England settlers wanted wealth and opportunity as much as any Europeans who emigrated to America. But they wanted something else as well. Initially, they had come to establish a Christian commonwealth, free of the corruptions they had found in Anglicanism. It was to be a model—a city upon a hill—which all the world could emulate. Community and order were central. All matters were calculated in terms of community cohesion and control. It was possible to survive the hardships of settlement, even surpass England in riches and wealth, yet fail dismally, if what they had created was a society in which men were spun off, free to do as they would.

The Puritan community was to be, as far as they could make it, orthodox in religious thought and practice, and homogeneous. That was the ideal, of course; it was unlikely to be realized. Quite early, the Puritans had to deal with centrifugal pressures, groups splitting away from specifc tenets of doctrine, spinning off into new towns. However imperfect, it was, nevertheless, a guiding principle.

Such a concern for community underlies the reason New Englanders were never persuaded to employ African slaves for profit. What would happen to the Christian commonwealth, the cohesiveness and order of the community, if large numbers of Africans were to abide among them? While the Virginia government, lacking much in the way of central town and village life, could leave the control, discipline, and morals of plantations to masters, nothing so important could be left to individuals in the Puritan settlement. The community would always have the burden of the morality and order of each household. Black slavery on a large scale could only corrupt everyone and everything.

That did not mean they thought slavery was evil in itself. Merchants were free to traffic in slaves, assuming them to be captives in just wars. And a number of black men and women were held as slaves in New England. But as Samuel Sewall argued in the first American anti-slavery tract, *The Selling of Joseph, a Memorial* (1700), Africans would not be content as slaves: they would want liberty among men who would not welcome them as citizens. They would not be allowed to take their place among the militia, nor would they be husbands to the daughters of the colony. They could not, like free men, be a part of the community, and as slaves they would covet freedom. So what would be the result of increasing their numbers except to invite disorder?

It is not strictly true that blacks were excluded from the duties of ordinary men in the sense of Samuel Sewall's argument. When need be, blacks were armed in the South to put down Indians. In Bacon's Rebellion, both Governor William Berkeley of Virginia and the rebel leader Nathaniel Bacon offered freedom to servants and slaves who would defend the one side or the other. Furthermore, white women and black men were known to have intermarried in the North and the South. But these were all exceptional cases.

Some colonies were becoming dependent on blacks, but nowhere was there a willingness to accept the fact of their presence as part of the organic community. Where Africans were needed in large numbers, they were insulated from society by the institution of slavery. Where blacks were not essential, it was largely because they were not wanted, and their numbers were kept small by slight encouragement for their employment.

When the colonies broke from England and cast themselves as one nation, the ambivalence over blacks and slavery was deep. The revolutionary rationale rested upon assumptions of irreducible human rights. Coming out of a state of nature, man had, by making a compact, vested power in the government, but his rights to life, liberty, and property were fixed in nature. Any government would be a tyranny if it usurped that natural endowment. But could men, thinking this, imagine that black men—their slaves—were somehow outside that formulation and were lacking in those natural rights?

The framers of the Virginia Bill of Rights found, for themselves, a way out. They wrote "that all men are by Nature equally free and independent, and have certain inherent Rights, of which they cannot by any Compact deprive or divest their Posterity." So they wrote at first. But, on second thought, with their black and Indian slaves in mind, they added after the word "which" the phrase "when they enter into a state of society."

It would seem that the Africans who had become their slaves and the Indians, enslaved or in the wilderness, had been arrested in a state of nature. All of the rationale of the Enlightenment, the theorizing of John Locke and Jean Jacques Rousseau, applied to "civilized" men and not to them.

That was one way to extricate themselves from the dilemma, but there were others. Those inherent rights, after all, were rights to life, liberty, and property. The slave was an anomaly. He was a man, it was true, but he was also the property of men. The Patriots had not created the institution, although they lived with it. If we are to believe men like George Washington, Thomas Jefferson, and James Madison, they would as soon slavery never existed in the country. Yet it was there: men who were the property of men. If it was tyranny to deprive a man of his liberty, it was no less so to take his property.

The dilemma should have been numbing, but it did not trouble the Founding Fathers enough to confront it. Natural rights theory served the cause of independence, and it gave white men a justification for disorder and, what was in effect, tyrannicide. Southerners, indeed, could take the lead in revolutionary rhetoric, for they, unlike Northerners, need not pause over the implications for their own lower orders. Slavery had made the primary social division racial rather than class. It would be much easier for a Thomas Jefferson or a Patrick Henry to slip into revolutionary rhetoric than it would be for John Adams.

Some slaves and free blacks were, themselves, caught up in the ideology of revolution. They tried to join the Continental Army, which was much against accepting them. Some managed to serve, nevertheless, and fought for their liberty that way. There were masters who chose to substitute slaves for themselves in the militia levies. Large numbers of blacks, slave and free, saw the chance for liberty on the British side, and they had

more than ideology to go on. The British offered freedom to the slaves of rebels who would serve the British
as spies, scouts, and servants. Most, however, sat tight
and awaited events.

With the war's end, liberty's triumph was uncertain
for blacks. Most of those who had served the American
side won their freedom. Those who went with the
British were evacuated with them. Many went to new
plantations in the West Indies, but some went to Nova
Scotia and, later, to the British African colony of Sierra
Leone, which was to become the nineteenth-century
West African haven for fugitives of the outlawed slave
trade.

The new government of the United States, struggling
to adjust its new relations with England, tried to exact
English compensation for American citizens whose
property had been confiscated by the British Army.
Since much of that property was in human beings, it
was an ignoble beginning for the land of the free.

Black people had no advocates in the councils that
created the new nation. From the documents, one would
hardly suspect that there was an enslaved or semi-free
population. The Constitution asserted that an unnamed
category of humanity—not free, not bound for a term
of service, not untaxed Indians—should count as three
fifths of a person for purposes of enumeration. It
alluded to an unnamed people who were presently
allowed to migrate into the country, protecting such
immigration until 1808, when these persons would be
subject to a tax of ten dollars each. It asserted that those
held to labor or service in one state could not escape
that status by fleeing to another where laws might differ,
but must be delivered up to the party claiming their
labor. Thus, in no way were the Founding Fathers direct or forthright about the peculiar racial and labor

system in the new country. Perhaps they were embarrassed for such matters to appear in the organic law establishing the model government against tyranny.

The Constitution was not to mean what it said, in general, when its principles were applied to black people. Certainly, blacks who enjoyed the status of citizenship in states like Massachusetts and New York would not be granted the privileges and immunities of the several states as the Constitution claimed. Furthermore, the federal government enacted fugitive slave laws that would deprive such persons of their liberty, if not their lives and their property, without what was understood to be due process of law.

While the federal Constitution, along with its Bill of Rights, became the model for the documents of many states, the guarantees against tyranny—the rights to freedom of speech, press, assembly, the free exercise of religion, the sanctity of contract (marriage, for instance), the protection against illegal search and seizure, the right to trial by jury with guarantee of counsel and the power to call witnesses, the right (if it did exist) to bear arms, the protection against cruel and unusual punishment—did not apply to slaves and, for the most part, did not apply to free blacks either.

The Constitution, however, did preserve slavery as it existed by its oblique recognition of the slave in fractional enumeration, by accepting in principle the right to import slave labor, by protecting slaves from effective escape into free states and territories, and by guaranteeing federal power to quash internal insurrections when asked by a state legislature or governor.

But the Constitution's strongest support for the permanence of slavery was in the federal system it constructed, for in that system of multiple sovereignties, the only jurisdictions that could effectively reform or abolish slavery were those where it existed. Since, in those states, the slaves' interests were not to be taken into account, and power was almost exclusively in the hands of those who profited from slavery, it would be unlikely that the state governments would be moved to reform. The Founding Fathers gave the central government enough power to protect slavery and the right of ownership in human property, but they refrained from giving it the means of abolition or reform. At least under the Articles of Confederation, which had governed the nation until 1789, each state could determine the degree to which it would participate in the support and protection of slavery. Given a slave insurrection in Virginia, Massachusetts might not be persuaded of the need to contribute to its suppression. The Constitution removed that choice, making all states supporters of the peculiar institution.

The framers of the Constitution seemed to foreshadow quite well the sense and mood of those who would lead the country in the half century that followed ratification. For while Congress was given some modest power that might have been used to affect slavery— regulation of interstate commerce and control over the District of Columbia—it failed to make anything of it. Congress did prohibit both the importation of slaves after 1808 and, as part of the Compromise of 1850, the slave trade in the District of Columbia. On the other hand, over time it strengthened and implemented the power of the government to apprehend fugitive slaves and return them to those claiming to own them. Congress never attempted to control or regulate the interstate traffic in slaves, without which the institution could not have survived.

Revolutionary idealism had its effect on slavery, however. Those states of New England, where there was

slight investment in slave property, were rather quick
to disavow the institution. While the sentiment against
slavery was strong in the states of New York, Pennsylvania, and New Jersey, abolishing the institution was a
longer and more troubling process.

Many Southern whites complained of the burden of
slavery on a generation that had not chosen it. George
Washington actually freed his slaves; Thomas Jefferson expressed regrets that he could not. Some thought
that in time slaves would become an economic burden
on their owners, who would be required to feed and
clothe them even in a feeble economy. But no one could
see a way out. They were unable to imagine a society of
free men that was mixed racially. With such irresolu-
tion, slavery persisted until revitalized in the late 1820s.

This same ambivalence about race and slavery went
westward with the nation. Under the Articles of Confederation, the government had designed the formula by
which the territory to the west of the Alleghenies and
north of the Ohio River would be organized into new
states. The Northwest Ordinance of 1787 was specific
in prohibiting there either slavery or involuntary servitude.

The whites who came from the South across the Ohio,
and from the Northeast over western New York and
Pennsylvania, echoed opinions held from the beginning
of the African migration. Some felt it an unfair burden
to be without slave labor to break up the new country.
Like Georgians earlier, they argued that the territories'
rapid development and potential wealth depended upon
the labor of enslaved blacks. On the other side, men
argued that slavery undermined free labor and the small
farmer, that it created unfair competition for those who
could not afford or were unwilling to own slaves. Furthermore, it obliged all free men to be actively engaged

in the maintenance of public order for the benefit of
those who held slave property. But, most of all, those
who would insist on the prohibition of slavery from the
territories echoed Samuel Sewall's contention that
blacks could not be accepted as part of the community;
they would be an unwanted and corrupting element.

As the states of Ohio, Indiana, and Illinois developed,
they followed the proscription of the Ordinance. More
than that, however, state legislatures and constitutional
revisions placed extraordinary restraints on free blacks
who might choose to settle there. Regulations made it
illegal for blacks to settle or hold property, and although
universal male suffrage became the rule in these new
states, blacks were not given the franchise. There would
be no slavery, but neither would blacks be welcome.

Westward expansion across the Southern frontier involved no restraints against slavery. Before the new
century opened, whites from Virginia, the Carolinas,
and Maryland brought their slaves across the mountains
into Kentucky and Tennessee. So, too, as land became
available through the incorporation of Spanish Florida,
the acquisition of French Louisiana, and the suppression and removal of Indians to the Trans-Mississippi
West, Georgia, Alabama, Mississippi, Arkansas, Missouri, and ultimately Texas were to be opened through
the power of slave labor.

Thus, the two paths of American community development regarding race, stemming from the earliest times
in the seventeenth century, were to extend themselves
throughout the continent. Blacks would be suitable instruments of development for the wealth of white men.
Or they would be unwelcome, excluded as far as that
might be possible. Either way, they would be outside
the community.

These two paths were antagonistic only in that they

would define the national future in opposing terms. Western lands would be open to Southerners and their slaves, or Southern whites would be denied free access to the nation's potential wealth. Those who saw themselves as free farmers felt their enterprise to be incompatible with the slave system. The territory to the west belonged to all white claimants regardless of their source of labor, or it would be reserved only to free farmers for their exploitation and development.

It was in the spirit of this conflict that James Tallmadge, Jr., a representative from New York, attempted in 1819 to amend the act that would enable Missouri to gain statehood, prohibiting the further introduction of slaves and providing for the gradual freeing of those blacks already there. The Tallmadge Amendment would oblige Missouri to follow the formula of the Northwest Ordinance. Was the entire Louisiana Purchase to be organized as had been the Old Northwest, or was this new country to be open for all white men to pursue their happiness?

The political compromise that allowed Missouri to remain open to slavery, that projected the state's southernmost border across the Louisiana Territory as a dividing line between that portion which could be organized for slavery and that which would remain free, merely formalized the two paths of racial accommodation. Further, it preserved the political balance in the Senate, serving to protect the interests of slaveholders.

The same formula was eagerly seized in 1850 as a means of solving identical organizational problems for territory taken in the Mexican War. It was grasping at straws by then, however. Slaveholders wanted the nation's future defined not merely to guarantee their right to hold human property but to allow them a free rein in exploiting the country. On the other hand, those who would call themselves Free Soilers would not presume to attack slavery where it existed but would insist that the new country was their oyster—for free white men only.

There was no one to argue for the right of Afro-Americans to exploit the territory for their own wealth or to be disencumbered of local restrictions against their residency, land ownership, and access to public resources. Such burdens were common across the free North, from New England to Oregon. The Afro-Americans' rights as a free people in a free country were never squarely addressed. While the Civil War, and the Reconstruction that followed, made it an unavoidable question, it was not confronted forthrightly even then.

As the nation developed, external threats to its order were reduced and, in time, eliminated. In the beginning, there were Spanish settlements to the south of the Carolinas and Georgia, French settlements to the west, and throughout the South and the Northwest a sizable Indian presence. French rule ended in 1803, Spanish Florida was incorporated into the United States in 1819, and following several Indian wars—culminating in a series of treaties in the 1830s—the Indians of the Old Southwest were forced to move to the plains west of the Mississippi.

Each incorporation or consolidation of territory into Anglo-American hands strengthened the hegemony of slave culture. As whites moved with their slaves into the West, they pressed ever more forcibly against borders that might have offered havens for black fugitives. Alien neighbors always fed fears of provoked slave uprisings. Mexico prohibited slavery, so Anglo-American settlers fomented rebellion, creating the Republic of Texas, which would be brought into the Union as a slave state.

The progress of the United States across the continent and the consolidation of its power reduced the practical options open to Afro-Americans, slave and free. By 1860, the American South, with its large unfree population, could no longer be considered, as it once might have been, the soft underbelly of the American nation. It was now insulated against foreign threats.

The westward expansion of the plantation system between 1815 and 1860 meant the forcible uprooting of hundreds of thousands of black men, women, and children. It was during this great migration that slave families were most likely to be broken up and kinfolk separated from one another forever.

The slave experience began as part of frontier life and would continue to be essential to the Southern frontier. Slavery and the breaking of new land created wealth for whites who settled and expanded across the South. From the colonial settlements on the Chesapeake to the newly opened country in Texas and Arkansas, a cycle of development repeated itself. White men with modest capital—title in land and ownership of a few slaves—would, on the labor of blacks, convert the wilderness tract into a producing enterprise. The country would be changed in a matter of decades into settled and richly productive farmland.

The destinies of black men and women on the Southern frontier were, even more than those of whites, a consequence of chance, for their master's luck was theirs as well. The plantation enterprise could grow grand or attain middling success, and the slaves' lives would be enhanced. But it was the nature of slavery that the range of benefits rewarding productive labor was narrow indeed.

They began as whites and blacks together, transform-

ing the untamed land into meager living space and a
money crop. Black men and women wielded broadax
and two-hand saw against standing timber. With white
men, they cut logs into their first dwelling place. Side
by side, they worked to clear enough land for first crops
of corn. They ate the same monotonous meals of cornmeal and salt pork, and they shared the same dirt floor
for a bed.

On the colonial frontier, whites depended on blacks
in their always uneasy contacts with Indians; often it
was blacks who came to know the inland rivers and
tapped the fur trade. When the delicate balance failed
between white men and red men, and war flared across
the land, blacks sometimes slipped away to exchange
their lot among whites for one among Indians, or they
joined their masters to defend what had been hacked
out of the wilderness by their sweat, creating a home
they shared.

The frontier threw the white man's dependency upon
blacks into naked relief. Isolated together, each could
find comfort in the other's strengths, welcome the
other's reliability. The common denominator of living
was the mutual need for survival in a country new to
both of them. In this closeness, black men could sense
in white men's needs a common humanity. They were
not equal—one was the other's servant and subject to
his will—but they were men together.

The frontier was fluid, and conditions and human
relationships transformed themselves as the country became settled and developed. The white man would bring
his woman: sometimes he had left his wife and children
until the place was ready; sometimes he found a chance
to marry a woman who would bring slaves, stock, and
land of her own.

The house would then need to be made larger, with

room for woman and family. The blacks would build cabins away from the master's house for themselves and new blacks who might come. If there had been a commonness of white and black, it now fell away. For the house they had shared, while primitive and modest, was the master's own house. Settled country meant a society for white people, and this would cause masters to draw away from the casual intimacies that had sustained them in meaner times.

The frontier experience was not pleasant for slaves. It entailed grueling work under conditions of great hardship. Dangers were all about: Indians; disease; wild animals and snakes, which grudgingly retreated from settled country. Survival could not be taken for granted among whites or blacks. It was the nature of slavery, however, that the risks to body and life all shared in the taming of the country would mainly profit the master, and what creature comforts came with the development would only incidentally enrich the slave.

The inevitable removal of master from slave was particlarly heightened by that crown of Southern evolution —the plantation. Its very organization left the master, even when in residence, removed from almost all primary, day-to-day contact with his slaves. The effects of this distancing were not, of course, all negative for the slave. Where the workings of a plantation were large enough for differentiation of tasks and roles, for a black population sufficiently large to create a self-sustaining life and culture away from white people's constant supervision, there could possibly grow a sense of a slave community. That would be an advantage of a sort.

As the American continent was developed and settled from the seventeenth century to the Civil War, black and white, master and slave, were to re-enact this drama of divorce. Each time, a different place, a different set of circumstances: the woodlands of Virginia and the Carolinas; the semi-tropical forests and marshes of Florida and southern Georgia, Mississippi, Louisiana, and East Texas; the upcountry of Tennessee and Kentucky, were all broken by the broadax and plow in the hands of black men and women. That had to be done before they could raise tobacco, rice, cotton, sugar, and hemp, producing the wealth on which the large estates of the Old South were based.

It was not unusual for a white man to begin with modest holdings of land and slaves and, with judicious marriage and good fortune, acquire more land and slaves until he was a substantial planter. His original slave workers would have increased their families in time, and he would be able to set up his white children in modest circumstances by gifts of slaves and land. Thus, a new cycle would commence, but at the expense of black families and kinship.

Slavery developed against a backdrop of American national expansion and political evolution. The Afro-American's unfreedom was different in the colonial South and New England; different as Southern agricultural enterprise carried it to the moving Southern frontier, across the mountains into Kentucky, down into new lands of the Deep South, across the Mississippi; different in tobacco, rice, or cotton; different in city or country; different in each specific place and time because each context would fix the terms in which unfreedom would be defined.

It was not merely that slaves were born into servitude in a free country that set them apart; that was odd enough. But the deeper meaning of their slavery was that with almost no exceptions, they had no choice of where, whom, or how they were to serve. Although some slaves were known to influence their sale so that they might remain with family or in a familiar neighborhood, or serve known and preferred masters, they were few and fortunate who could so effect events. Such matters were out of the hands of most slaves, and even where they might presume to ask, the choice was absolutely at the owner's will. Whether the enterprise to which the slave gave his labor was thriving or failing, lush or churlish, was outside his ability to determine. Whether a slave was a part of a settled, older region or an element in the expanding frontier was also out of his hands. In every way, life in America for the slave was not rife with possibility but narrowly circumscribed and determined.

On a small operation, where the owner had few slaves and small acreage, it was a constant struggle merely to hold on or, beyond that, to grow, adding labor and land. Either way there was a great uncertainty, because there was little margin and failure in weather and crops could be devastating. The white man might well be in debt for land, supplies, or seed; and, as the farm and the blacks on it were his most likely collateral, his failure would fall upon them. For with a foreclosure, they would again be placed on the market block to be sold. It was at such times that slave families were most likely to be scattered.

To be a slave of a small landholder meant a life of narrowness and monotony geared to the landholder's means. Blacks might be made to eat outside the house or after the white man's family, but it was the same fare: cornmeal, pork, and molasses. Lacking quarters, the few slaves huddled in the corners of the white man's house. Lacking a mule, the slave would be lashed to the plow, pulling it before the white man over his fields. If the blacks were not themselves a family group, they would need the white man's permission to visit slaves on neighboring places for social life. And if one took a neighbor's slave for husband or wife, one could only hope the white man would be liberal enough to allow nightly visits or pray that he would buy one's family.

A little of everything was done on a small place, such as carpentry and animal care, but the primary focus was servicing a cash crop. Nothing much could be done that required special skills, like coopering, wheelwrighting, smithing, or milling. Thus, the slave stood little chance of gaining skills beyond that of field hand. His value lay in that and in his strength as long as it lasted.

When the enterprise grew to more than twenty-five slaves, the character of the slave's life changed. At this scale and larger, masters tended to pass direct management of labor to others. A white overseer would be hired, and he and his family would constitute a third element between master and slave. It was a troublesome addition all around, because the overseer had responsibility for the smooth, productive working of the place, but he did not have unqualified authority. Masters were seldom pleased, and slaves were often successful in undermining the overseer's power.

The division of labor became more intricate as the size of the plantation grew. A general domestic staff evolved into house servants with special skills—cooks, waiters, maids, and valets. In the most magnificent places, these servants were highly skilled, elegant in livery. The master's house was large, with space enough for some black servants to sleep within. In this was the first possibility of separation of domestics from field servants as a class. Such grand estates, however, remained few in number. The vast majority of slaves lived on modest plantations where fine divisions between domestics and field hands, skilled and unskilled, could not be achieved or supported.

A few large establishments could be self-contained, having within themselves resources to satisfy all needs. Labor thus refined itself into skills: carpenters, coopers, blacksmiths, wheelwrights, cobblers, as well as plowmen in the fields, cooks for slaves, and nurses for children and the infirm. In the rice country of South Carolina and Georgia, there needed to be persons skilled in the management of the dikes and dams, which flooded the fields, and the mills, which hulled the grain. In tobacco, the plants needed almost personal care while growing, and persons had to become skilled at curing, cropping, and packing the leaf. In sugar, the refineries on the plantations required technical skills, as did the gin mills on cotton plantations.

Agriculture and the farmer's relationship to his product developed differently in America from Old World practices. The American colonies were a part of a world-wide mercantile network; their very existence rested upon their ability to produce commodities for exchange in a market far removed from the products' source. In the Old World of Europe and Africa, the market had always played a part in the peasant's life, but the principal and immediate concern of any farmer was the subsistence of his family through his labor on the land.

When his labors produced more than he was obliged to pay in rents and more than the household could consume, he traded the surplus for things he did not have, foods he did not grow, and utensils and tools he did not make, or he might take gold as a means of future exchange.

In America, things were reversed. From the beginning, the European settlers looked toward commerce
first. Virginians even suffered on the margin of survival
as their energies went into discovering a product suitable for commerce and profit. They hit upon tobacco,
which could neither be eaten nor put on one's back.
Settlers along the coasts of South Carolina and Georgia
produced rice, and Louisiana planters sold sugar for an
international market. In time, cotton would surpass all
these as the major crop in the slave states. But there
would be other regional specialties. From the pine
forests, turpentine, tar, pitch, and rosin; from Kentucky, hemp for bagging and rope.

All of these commercial products meant a divorce-
ment of people's labor from their needs. Africans, like
other peasant folk, had an immediate sense of how
energy and labor converted into food and necessities.
The peasant farmer grew what he ate; the energy of his
body was directly tied to what went into his stomach,
on his back, and over his head. But the care and labor
that went into tobacco, rice, sugar, or cotton would exchange for so much credit in terms of money and
thereby would also determine how much one's labor
was worth and, incidentally, how much a black man,
woman, or child would exchange for in the market. The
slave felt the effects when the market for the staple rose
or declined—whether he would be sold from tobacco,
where the price was low, and bought in cotton, where
the market was rising—but his labor, skills, and character had little or nothing to do with this strange and abstract value system.

Had it not been foretold in Africa? For there, too,
the African's worth became a matter of a distant market
—what London merchants were paying for tobacco,

rice, and sugar would determine what an African would be worth in America.

This was a profound change in the sense of labor on the land. For the white owners, it meant management of land and labor with an eye to the market value of the commodity rather than to the resource itself. The peasant preserved his land, his stock, and his tools, for they were his only resources, convertible into nothing else. The planter knew that with money or credit he could replace land and even labor, if need be. Perhaps he would not willfully destroy his land (although many seemed to have done that) or his slaves; but the common-sense argument that a man would not intentionally ruin his property in slaves by brutality missed the point that it might be economically sound to do that if the market price of the staple was right.

For the African, commerce drove a wedge between what were, traditionally, related elements: his labor, its product, and his well-being. His hand turned the soil and urged it to bring forth a fruit that he could eat and which only in an indirect way would support him. What he ate and what he wore varied little with the diligence of his labor or the quality of the crop. He lived on a margin in fat years and lean. Except for those few who worked farms that produced corn and wheat, and raised livestock for the market, there was none of the goodness of life in his work. It would have been the same had he been a factory worker rather than a farmer. The commercial emphasis of the American farm and the Southern plantation transformed blacks and whites into elements of industry, tied to factors of commerce.

Some slaves' work was far removed from peasant work: they were pulled into the labor of a growing commercial society. Even the produce of plantations required nonfarm workers: carpenters, housewrights, coopers. Rice required modest civil engineering; the rice, which was once cleaned by the African-style mortar and pestle, in time needed the skills of mechanics on new machines, as did the mills of the sugar plantations, which converted the juices of cane into syrup and sugar, and the mills that ground corn and wheat into meal and flour. Black workers converted hemp into sacking and rope, animal hides into leather, pressed tobacco into bulk form. They ginned and baled cotton, salted and cured meats.

Black men worked underground in mines extracting coal, lead, and gold; and in tunnels that railroads would need. They worked the railroads of the South—doing all of the construction and grading for laying track, then staffed the system as firemen, brakemen, and engineers. They worked on building the canals, which linked waterways to one another. They pulled the barges through those canals. They sailed on the steamers and keelboats that plied the Ohio, Missouri, and Mississippi Rivers, and up into the Chesapeake waterways. They worked on the wharves of river cities like Louisville, St. Louis, and Memphis. They served as stevedores at seaports and gulf ports like New Orleans, Mobile, Savannah, Charleston, and Baltimore, and many of the coastwise ships that used those ports had slaves and free blacks among the crew.

Slaves were lumbermen. They cleared forests, cutting trees into beams, milling them into planks and lumber. They drained sap from the pines, distilled it into turpentine, watched the slow fires that converted the desiccated trees into tar and pitch. They did the quarry work: drilled and tapped the explosives, cut and polished the stone, and freighted it away. When Southerners built textile mills, black men and women worked the looms. Slaves were the bone and sinew of iron mining and manufacturing in the South. The roads, the levees, and the public ways of the South were built and maintained by black hands.

Many of the slaves who worked in such industry were hired out by their owners for a fee. Most of the labor was arduous and much more dangerous than farm work at its worst. Seldom could such industrial workers have a settled place and family; and except for a large male society in most of these industries, there was no social life. Many worked six, sometimes seven days a week, often working in two shifts of twelve hours each.

Because there were slaves in Southern industry, there were slaves in Southern cities. Most were domestic servants of white city dwellers or planters who had townhouses. But many also made up the work force of the Southern cities: draymen, stevedores, carpenters, masons, and common laborers.

Urban life was more varied than rural, so blacks as well as whites enjoyed a more liberal environment. As there was a wider variety of enterprises, slaves were not singularly dependent upon the life of their particular household. There were free blacks as well as slaves, and a social life that extended beyond one's masters' control. While cities had rules against the assembly of blacks, they were difficult to enforce, enabling blacks to congregate, gossip, share stories, find friends, and plot.

Slaves' housing in cities tended to be attached to that of their owners, which would mean more comfortable and livable quarters than those in the country. The markets offered a wider selection of foods and other goods than could be obtained in the country. Especially in the seaport towns, there would be seafood in abundance and goods imported from abroad. Most slaves could find some way to hire out their time or convert

something into money, so it was possible to enrich their
diet or improve their clothing or enjoy themselves in
the hidden places where liquor could be had.

It was difficult to stifle the freer atmosphere of the
city. Slaves could not be kept from the knowledge that
freedom was a real possibility for them, since they were
in constant touch with free blacks. They could not be
kept from learning to read or learning of the world outside. And occasionally, there would come a chance to
stow away on a boat that could take one out of slavery
forever.

America moved inexorably to close itself off as a
slave society. Although it began with uncertainty and
ambiguities, in time it came to understand itself as a
society of white men who would use blacks as slaves
or not welcome them. There had been challenges early
on: alien claimants to the frontier—Indian, Spanish,
French, Mexican.

For black Americans, there had seemed several ways
out in the beginning. Conversion to Christianity could
win freedom among some masters. But that was soon
ended. Escape across the frontier to non-English peoples was, in time, shut off by the westward expansion
of the Anglo-American nation. By the 1840s, slavery
was the way of life of the Southern states of the United
States, and there would be slight chance to get out of it.

There had once been dissent by Southern whites.
Until the 1830s, whites in the South raised their voices
against owning human property. They would urge upon
the society ways to do away with slavery, including
transporting blacks to Africa. But their voices were
muted or silenced. Those who persisted were intimi-
dated, their presses were smashed, and they were forced
to leave the South. While slavery—"our peculiar insti-

tution"—would remain the major topic of conversation among Southerners, criticism was not to be tolerated.

Even those slaveholders who wished to free their slaves would find it harder to do so as time went on. By the mid-nineteenth century, it was nearly impossible. Most states forbade manumission within the state, so owners wishing to free their slaves would need the foresight to carry them to Northern states. Even wills leaving such instructions often fell under the challenges of claimants at probate.

By the mid-1830s, free blacks, not slaves, were the anomaly in the South. New slave states denied them a place at all. In the older states, where a free black population dated from the seventeenth century, they were so circumscribed and harassed that their condition was in constant jeopardy.

The vigilance of Southerners in the protection of slavery was undeterred by concern for civil liberties, even those of whites. Newspapers and pamphlets were scrutinized for subversive notions. Mails in the United States post offices were confiscated if they were thought to be inciteful. Restrictions against slaves learning to read or preaching the gospel or meeting together were enforced with growing intensity. Ironically, even the prohibition against the importation of slaves in 1808— that law thought to be an act against slavery—served to shut off Afro-Americans from the continued stimulus of new Africans among them.

Southern society had become a monolith, resting upon the single object of preserving and justifying its "peculiar institution." Nothing could come before it. Its economy rested on the enslavement of blacks, who had no say in how they were governed. The men who did govern were those served by the slave system, and the laws they enacted supported that interest without

qualification. All Southerners, white and black, slave
and free, were controlled by the rationalization of
slavery's protection. Blacks were presumed unfree without positive proof to the contrary. Whites were con-
scripted into slave patrols to keep order among slaves,
whether they had a property interest in them or not.

Here was a model totalitarian society supported directly or indirectly by the entire nation. From the perspective of the Afro-American, the United States, by
the eve of the Civil War, was what the Founding
Fathers meant when they described tyranny.

5

Master and Slave

To the African mind, unfreedom was no outlandish condition. Freedom was not much thought about in the Old World. One always belonged to a place and a people, having ties and obligations going far beyond the will of a single person to change. Imagining a state of freedom—meaning to be unfettered by wills, judgments, and determinations not one's own—would have been a frightening vision, like being a plant with roots in the earth too shallow to hold fast, like being free to move in the wind but having no place and no way to draw sustenance.

American slavery, however, required a radical transformation of personal meaning. In the New World, one asked "What is a person worth? What is his value?" That would have been a strange question to Africans before the slave trade. To them, a person was, he belonged, he had meaning—be he powerful or weak, quick or slow. But they would have been at a loss to discover a quantitative value to stand for a man or woman. That is not to claim that the African held indi-

vidual human life in higher esteem than did Europeans.
There was human sacrifice, of course, and the close
margins of life and death served to inure them to personal loss. It was, merely, that the estimate of human
quality would not have been calculated in money, goods,
or as capital assets.

But, in essence, that was what American slavery was
all about. It began in the African slave markets, and
Afro-American generations to come would know the
market to be the social test of their value. To be felt and
inspected, talked of as a thing, transferred from place
to place, bought and sold—that was the common pulse
of the slave experience through two and one half centuries of Afro-American history.

Even those few fortunate enough never to hear the
auctioneer chant their qualities would know the slave
market as the basic symbol of their condition. Boys of
a certain age went for so much, able-bodied, mature
men for another amount. Acquired skills added to the
price; marks from the lash took value away. Strong-
bodied women who could fell trees and plow commanded one price; frail or sickly ones brought less. A
comely young woman in the flush of youth might send
prices beyond reasonable bounds. Did a woman have
children? Would she have more? There was money in
that. Did a man have the marks from smallpox? That
was value to the discerning eye.

To be chattel property meant one could be traded
and transferred as any other object of value. A master
who wanted to set his children up on their own normally did so with a gift from among his own slaves,
often breaking black kinship ties as a result. In fact, in
the antebellum United States, which lacked a national
monetary system, where state and private bank notes
were insecure and lost value at a distance from place of

issue, slaves were a convenient way to move wealth from one state to another.

One was a thing to be bought and sold, traded for money, land, or other objects. One was a living animal —like a horse, a cow, a pig—so that one's seed was part of the bargain. To Euro-Americans, the slave was like livestock but with a crucial difference: the slave was a responsible creature. He was no mere trained animal able only to respond to signals. He was a thinking, moral being; he was assumed to know right from wrong. Unlike a horse or cow or pig, he could do evil and assume the weight of his behavior. The society that enslaved him understood this difference, holding him strictly to the law for his misdeeds. A pig in the corn was not a thief; a slave in the smokehouse was. A horse that trampled the life from a cruel master was no murderer; a slave who struck out against brutality was. While the slave was a thing to be traded in the market, all depended upon his being human as well.

The slave had a human intelligence; that was an element of his price in the market. The Africans had brought techniques for growing crops, raising livestock, building dwellings, preparing food, weaving baskets, working metals, carving boats, netting fish, and trapping animals. Some of this lore would abide for generations after Africa had become a vague and dreamlike past. As they had retained old work skills, they would learn new ones. They continued to grow rice, indigo, watermelons, and cotton, but they learned to handle crops, like sugar and corn, that were new both to them and the Europeans. Workers familiar with hoes, casting nets, and looms also adjusted to a variety of European tools that were put into their hands. The white man recognized and profited from these capacities, even as he denied their existence. The slave could plan, organize, and direct as well as the master, perhaps better. In that way the slave would be more valuable, more useful, but also more threatening, for as the slave came to understand how little stood between his master and himself, his imagination would certainly conspire to find ways to defy the market system.

Euro-Americans and Afro-Americans seemed to have understood from the beginning that they shared a common humanity; both were different from animals and things. As this was presumed in moral capacity and intelligence, so it was also witnessed in the gratification that each could find in the other. White men had taken black women on the slave coast as well as in the middle passage. In the early colonial years, when white and black servants were often comrades, it was not uncommon for black men and white women, as well as white men and black women, to become sexual partners and "marry." Mulatto offspring would attest to this. Authority never liked the practice, and its censure was likely to use the word "unnatural" as rhetoric. However, it could never have been more of a crime than fornication or adultery, both natural enough. It would never have been considered as sodomy or bestiality.

The governing authorities of the Southern colonies had many reasons to discourage miscegenation, and they passed laws against it. While white men were never really prohibited from finding their pleasure with black women, rigorous penalties—for the men, death, maiming, castration; for the women, social ostracism—limited black men from consorting as frequently with white women. However, despite the increasingly elaborate rhetoric and legislation of the master class, all knew well enough that truly "unnatural acts" would not have needed such proscription.

It was a troubling matter to have a marketable commodity who was also human, for the owner could never be wholly free to treat this human being as a thing, and the slave could never be wholly convinced that his human quality did not imply being something more than an object of other people's needs. The disparities abounded. How could one who was not his own master be responsible for his acts? How could one's property be the parent of one's own sons and daughters, who were, themselves, one's chattel?

The dilemma was especially vexing in a society supposedly based on human rights. No one claimed that property had vested rights, but everyone knew human beings did: it was a self-evident truth. Logic would have it one way or the other: either these black people were human and could not be property, or they were property and something less than human.

Many would want to resolve the dilemma, assuming blacks to be less than human. From the first contacts, the differences had seemed striking: color, religion, customs. Certainly that sense of difference gave a predisposition for bigotry. But it was the experience of slavery itself—the living together as master and slave, oppressor and oppressed—and the exclusively racial definition of that status that converted Euro-American prejudice, bigotry, and ethnocentrism into something more sinister, where, because of race, men and women were excepted from normal human considerations.

As time passed, it was not the differences between the races that became crucial. It would not have been difficult to explain special treatment for an exotic and threatening people. It was, rather, the sameness that was the problem. The more white and black, master and slave, shared the same culture, spoke the same language, were tied by kinship and custom, birthplace and lifestyles, the greater the need for a rationale to justify distinctions and to deny to the one what the other claimed as his natural right.

Laws and customs pushed blacks beyond obligatory immunities. They were not persons in any sense the law need recognize. They could not be contracting parties: their marriages and other agreements had no binding force other than what would suit the convenience of whites. Their word and their witness would not be accepted in official business concerning white men. They had no recourse in the case of injury to their persons or their families, no guarantee of protection for what they might come to possess. Their principal security lay in their master's indulgence, not in the community as expressed by law.

White men searched desperately for differences which could justify an exploitation that went counter to principles. They turned to the Bible's story of Ham's curious offense against his father, which doomed his tribe to servitude. But nothing in that story claimed that Ham's children were different from other humans. Other white men wanted the Bible to say that God had created different types of men, and only white men were the legitimate children of God; Africans, Asians, and American Indians were lesser creatures. The Bible was not really helpful for this purpose, especially among white Protestants, whose fundamentalist notions of scripture ran too deep for them to accept such liberties with Genesis.

During the nineteenth century, the new sciences of ethnology and anthropology offered better opportunities, especially as little literature existed to contradict speculation. There was great room for tendentious conjecture in the name of empirical investigation. Medical doctors claimed physiological and psychological characteristics peculiar to blacks. Slave behavior that did not contribute to the master's interests—"laziness,"

feigned illness, sabotage, escape—was given impressive
Latin names as specific "diseases" said to be "peculiar
to Negroes." In the early decades of the nineteenth century, some Euro-American scientists, known as "the
American School," measured the size and shape of
human skulls and claimed to have discovered a difference in favor of Europeans over all other peoples.
Rather than *Man*, these scientists argued, there were
Types of Mankind forming an ascending chain from the
lower animals and primates. The closest to the ape were
blacks, and at the apex of nature's achievement were
white men. In response to questions of how truly different species can mate to produce offspring, they
quickly pointed out that horses and donkeys could produce mules, so whites and blacks could produce mulattoes. And to those who would argue that mules were
sterile as a result of such cross-breeding while mulattoes
could reproduce, they claimed that mulattoes were
"weaker" than their parents and within a few generations they, too, would be sterile.

Black men and women were unlikely to know of such
"science." Only a few whites, for that matter, would be
acquainted with these theories, and only a handful of
those would take them seriously. But both blacks and
whites could understand what these speculations reflected. In the United States, it was so much more convenient for blacks to be considered less human than
whites that it set the tide against all reason, logic, and
empirical observation.

Afro-Americans, as slaves, swam against that current,
defying it and in many ways overcoming it. That is why
they were troublesome property. Not only did they revolt, escape, and otherwise resist enslavement, but even
in accommodating, they maintained their human quality.

Some white owners responded to this dilemma with

human accommodations of their own. Rather than hold
to the property side, they would enhance personal relationships, making their slaves part of the family (which,
as a matter of fact, they sometimes were); they would
hold them as trusted friends. But this behavior worked
only insofar as such whites and their slaves could insu-
late themselves from the exigencies of the system.
Whenever there was cause to go outside private understandings and to touch base with public expectations,
the property would be reasserted as the hard ground on
which all stood.

Just as it was not the fact of unfreedom that was unnatural about slavery in America, it was not the condition of inequality that was disturbing. Both Europeans
and Africans had lived in societies that assumed superiors and inferiors in all human relationships. If anything, the notion that all men were equal went against
observed experience and common sense.

Africans, as much as Europeans, were an aristocratic
people. Inequalities were perceived as natural and expected, and deference was readily given to acknowledged superiors. One dropped to one's knees before
one's father and elders. One called one's social superior
"master." Such inequalities were normally sustained
and justified in an organic social context that served as
a corrective against arbitrary distinctions. Ability, age,
wisdom, and the force of character or personality were
distinguishing features in most African societies.

But what made whites the masters and superiors of
blacks was power—not individual power, but a social
and collective power that had little to do with their
worth as people. Initially, it was a superior technology
in weapons and ships. In America, it was the owner's
ability to inflict pain and death with the entire coercive

power of the state behind him, for if his personal power was not enough, the state would stand in his stead to subdue challenges from slaves.

For the slaves, there were narrow choices. They could defy power, removing themselves from its sway by escape or death, or resign themselves to the fact of overwhelming power against them. Within their acquiescence there was a range of patterns from the edge of defiance to abject sycophancy. Accommodation under such circumstances, however, no more denoted legitimacy than would any other survival method under tyranny.

The absoluteness of force in the master's hands was a matter of public display. Strung up to trees, staked out on the ground, held down by others, stripped to the bare flesh, slaves were beaten with every variety of instrument from whips to blunt weapons. They were subjected to pain so that it not only seared their own flesh but that their cries would make the skin of others crawl. They were branded, maimed, dismembered, and killed in full view of others. Such force was not only a deterrent; it was a ready and dramatic show of authority, a reminder of the juxtaposition of unmitigated power against unrelieved helplessness. There was hardly a slave who did not as an adult suffer the lash. Even those who would be gratified that their own master was unwilling to use the whip had a vivid sense of it from their neighbors.

Slaves could not have been unmindful of the arbitrariness of such power in a master's hands. Being a master had nothing to do with personal achievement, intelligence, or superiority of character. For the most part, one needed only to be white and have money or an inheritance. Masters could be incompetent, psychotic, perverted, and brutal, or gentle, sane, and intelligent. Slaves knew all ranges and types of human frailty in owners, and bore the good or ill luck that put them where they were.

But, of course, Euro-Americans need not be masters to be agents of the system and be superior to blacks. Non-slaveholding whites commonly made up the patrols that were the arm of community power against slaves. Confronted with the ever-present threat of violence from the broader society—the patrols and agents of the law—the slave had to rely on the power of his master to protect him. He was fortunate if he belonged to an influential owner who was willing to stand up for him. What ignominy to be the property of a person who had power only over black people and none among whites.

In a social and economic arrangement that could make no claim to justice, force was the sole means of maintaining peace and order, and the only instrument through which masters, and all whites for that matter, could remain superior to slaves and blacks. Yet, it was not enough to coerce black men and women into an unfree and oppressed condition; it was essential to have the whole system work as a productive enterprise. Slaves had to produce tobacco, rice, cotton, sugar, iron; build railroads and houses and levees. They must work efficiently from sunup to sundown, and force was the means of setting the terms between acceptable and unacceptable productivity.

The conversion of a peasant people to the discipline of industrial labor (for Southern agriculture was just that) has always been traumatic, requiring some compulsion. In normal societies, the compulsion was starvation: one worked according to a regimen or one did not eat. In the slave system, however, the master was bound to his labor by ownership. The goad of hunger could not work because it undermined the quality of his property and diminished its capacity to produce. Violence, and the threat of violence, was the alternative.

In personal interaction between master and slave, the naked reality of force could be mitigated. Both blacks and whites of sensibility would prefer to imagine that their relationship rested on something more legitimate than the monopoly of violence in the master's hands. Slaves became competent at certain tasks and were proud of their skills. It was possible to think—when encouraged to—that the relationship was founded on a mutual respect. Owners indulged the belief that their slaves were of their family, and many of their slaves appreciated and reciprocated that affection. Some whites and blacks were able to relate to one another as partners (albeit unequal) in a common enterprise. There were many such accommodations throughout the history of slavery in America. At their best they attest to the instinct for constructing human relationships even against the current of an oppressive system. But when we read the words of the whites and blacks who felt these relationships to be genuine, we are hard pressed to believe it more than sentimentality, for we know too well how unstable such feelings were when reality closed in.

The owner's needs might oblige him to hire out or to sell even the most valued slave. A wish to marry, to visit one's spouse, or to purchase one's freedom could expose the shallowness of the owner's love and respect. The master might will his slaves protection after his death, guaranteeing their good position, holding their families intact, granting them promised freedom. But such a will, as the owner himself understood, would not rest on assumed family feeling but on probate laws respecting the transfer of property in an estate. The master's white kin could well struggle to gain from his death, thereby thwarting his will. His creditors had claims that the law must honor, and there were laws limiting what one could do for the benfiit of slave property. Even the most genuine "family feeling" might endure for only the life of one man or one woman.

Whites and blacks both had their illusions nevertheless. Blacks sometimes relied heavily on a belief in the love expressed by their masters. But all too often they found it hollow, as their owners buckled under the system's pressures, giving in to open duplicity or proving powerless to effect their desires. In any event, it could be a shattering blow. Whites, too, accepted the warmth and intimacy of propinquity and good manners as love and affection on the part of some black person, and sometimes it was. But they might find the most trusted, beloved black suddenly escaped or insisting on his freedom or, when the time came, run off to join the Union Army. Such betrayal! Such ingratitude!

For a time whites and blacks were capable of indulging the other's fiction, that whatever others did or whatever the facts beyond them, they were friends whose relationship stemmed from love and respect. But these heroic efforts at humanity were, by necessity, epiphenomenal. Like ephemeral bubbles on a sea whose tides move by inexorable force, they foamed for their moment and then were gone. Everything else moved with the dominant current of an economic and social system.

Before every other consideration, the relationship between master and slave was an economic one, that between capitalist manager and labor. The ultimate end and rationale of the slave system was to make the enterprise work to the profit of the owner. Slaves were like land and stock, resources to be exploited and calculated in business judgments. Many masters and slaves shunned such crass descriptions of their relationships. As has often been the case among entrepreneurs, craftsmen, and workers caught in the early traumas of industrialization, they preferred not to discuss their human relationships and economic dependency in terms of mere efficiency and barter on the market. They liked better to talk of families, mutual obligations, paternalism, and *noblesse oblige*. But at bottom, such indulgence rested on the ability of the enterprise to flourish, and the master would certainly convince himself that it served no one's interest if his plantation failed to make money. Slaves must be productive for their own good as well as for his profit.

The master's role was managerial. Like other farmers he had to make calculations about how to employ his land and labor as well as his stock: how and when to clear land for planting, how much and what acreage to keep fallow, how much and when to invest in capital equipment (more slaves, animals, plows, gins, or mills), how to choose and control an overseer. Still, much was out of his hands to control: early frosts; weather too dry or too wet; sudden illness or epidemics among his workers; a fire in his mill or storehouse, which could wipe out large chunks of investment; the price the cash crop commanded on the distant market, which could reduce his best efforts to nothing. Thus, although some of his success or failure depended upon his management and judgment, much else was luck.

His most vexing problems would be in the proper management of his slaves. Disciplining them to efficient production required difficult decisions. Putting sentiment aside, one could make costly mistakes by being lenient or strict at the wrong time. It was true that most slaves could do more than they were apt to admit, but to force work at the wrong time might ruin a hand for good. Some women could work in the fields late into their pregnancy, whereas others were sickly and likely to miscarry with the slightest exertion. Obviously, one could not be absolute in determining who should work and how much. Yet, there was always the suspicion that one was being deceived and tested to see what the boundaries were. As a general rule, masters found hardness to be their best policy, for although there was the risk of prolonging or worsening an illness or even turning a curable malady into a fatality, it would be far more disruptive for slaves to think that complaints or feigned illness would get them out of work.

The long day was arduous and taxing. While most labor in the fields did not require a high level of skill, it did demand care and thoroughness. Careless plowing could ruin animals or equipment; improperly turned soil would have to be plowed again, wasting time. In crops like tobacco, each plant needed attention, the breaking off by hand of the suckers that would take from the large leaf. In cotton, there was the continuous need to chop away the young shoots from the desired and maturing stand. Great intensity of labor came seasonally; in sugar, for example, all the cane had to be cut, run through crushers, and milled in about ten weeks. At such times, breaks in discipline could mean disaster to the crop and the year's production.

Slave labor was driven labor, and slaves were trained into routines. Some masters chose to assign tasks of varied amounts of work to individuals. Men and women in their prime were considered full hands and given equivalent tasks. Children old enough to work in the fields but not yet at their full growth were considered part hands and given lesser tasks, as were the old and infirm. Other slave owners preferred a gang system, where platoons of hands would be worked in the fields under the eyes of drivers or overseers. The task system was best suited to crops like tobacco and rice, and gangs worked better in sugar and cotton.

Getting his slaves to produce was only part of the problem of managing them. The master had also to sustain their labor at a cost that would be worth his while. He had to feed, clothe, and house them, and service their health well enough to keep them fit for work— all at a cost that would leave him a margin for profit and growth. He fed them cornmeal, salt pork, and molasses. He gave them yearly allotments of clothes: shoes for adults, pants and shirts for men, dresses for women, linsey-woolsey long shirts for children (those who did not go naked), and blankets when needed.

It was marginal subsistence at best. It can be said that middling whites and some masters ate little better. But this fatty and starchy diet was barely supportive of health. Slaves supplemented it by tending small gardens of their own, so far as masters would allow, or by hunting, fishing, or stealing.

Operating within such narrow paths, slaves had their own needs to satisfy. Like other industrial workers, there was only a very indirect connection between their labor and their reward. The efforts put into a crop, unless in their own gardens, did not feed them or their families, nor did it relate to the clothing they put on their backs. They would know years in which the cotton, tobacco, rice, or sugar was lush and abundant, and they would know seasons when scarcely anything came from the land. While they were bound to suffer the master's failures—to be dislodged, moved, or sold—the margin on which they survived changed little in good years or bad. Thus, they were not very likely to think of their own productivity as having much to do with their survival or comfort.

True, if their work displeased their master or overseer, they were made to suffer. But they were not inclined to think: "If I work harder or more carefully, or if I plan better, I will get more of what I want." Theirs was a marginal existence, and their labor was to be marginal as well. The trick was to find the level of effort that would cause the least pain.

Yet there were personal concerns in which the slave might hope good treatment would follow good service. Primary, of course, was family life. The recognition of marriages by the master was crucial. With a spouse on a neighboring plantation, the master would have to sanction visits. If one was to be sold, he hoped that he would be kept near his family and friends. It would be nice to have the master's authority against white men who could interfere in family life.

Slaves with skills liked to sell their labor from time to time so that they might get money, clothes, or food. Others wanted to sell the produce of their gardens for their own benefit. Slaves came to expect Sundays off, to see it as a day when they could work in their gardens and care for their own domestic concerns. Holidays, especially Christmas, were almost everywhere occasions for parties and entertainment. There would be extras like whisky and cake and dances.

Individual slaves sought variety in work experience. There was pleasure and pride in taking up new and challenging tasks. Caring for animals, carpentry, smithing, and other activities made for more independent work than that in the fields and carried some authority too. The same can be said for being brought into the big house as a domestic servant, although that had the drawback of being too much under the eyes of white folks.

Of course, the most immediate benefit the slave could want was to be treated well, with kindness and consideration, to be respected and liked.

All of these matters were, in the slave's mind, compensation as food and clothing. While slaves thought a lot about food, especially that outside normal rations, these small considerations made the difference between existence and living with some human quality. But these matters were not so much tied to the slave's productivity as they were to the master's good will. Certainly, production affected the master's humor, but the slave had good reason to believe that pleasing the master, ingratiating oneself to him, was a more direct route to better treatment than harder and more efficient work.

The master had two basic strategies to achieve production and peace. Both required him to strike the style of tyrant: the tough autocrat or the benevolent despot. The one might well be moved to excesses of brutality; the other would indulge his feelings of family. The one could ignore neither the whip nor the auction block; the other would do well to keep his slaves alive and fit to work.

Slaves who would manipulate the system and even modestly improve their lot had only to know that ultimate authority rested with the master and his family. Laws might prevent a master from freeing his slaves or allowing them to run about as if they were free; patrols might harass his slaves even on his property; social gossip might make his name a scandal abroad. But the master's yea or nay remained the slave's principal concern, which made matters both easier and harder. There was no corporate or bureaucratic friction that could diffuse authority. Power was naked and direct. A man could make a decision, then change his mind on a whim, and the right persuasion could help. The clever slave needed only to know his master. It did not matter if he was a mean autocrat or a benevolent despot: he would be vulnerable to those who knew his character and how to exploit it. But, as masters differed in personality, slaves did too. All styles of manipulation did not suit every slave.

Children began at a young age to fawn and celebrate the master and his family when they would come among them. The white family would be surrounded by little black children—barefoot and dressed in only the slightest garments—greeting "massa" and "missus," telling them of their wonder and joy in seeing them, telling them of things they could do, begging sugar or sweets or treats, hanging about underfoot, with incessant chatter until they were chased away.

Some white folks complained about the ceaseless begging and cajoling, but most were really pleased by it, as it gave them a sense of their "family's" dependency on them. For the slave child, however, it was education in the manipulation of white people. The practice identified the central authority and exposed the peculiarities of his personal patience and tolerance. How much begging would win a treat? At what point was his impatience likely to produce a gift? Where would it bring anger instead? These were important calculations for slaves who would have to deal in this manner with one white person or another all their lives.

Such childhood begging was good training for the ingratiating style that could move masters and their wives. Master and servant found each other's depths and worked together as a tandem. Many whites who complained of the servants who whined, begged, or cajoled nevertheless always had such servants. A servant might begin his campaign days or even weeks ahead to gain his object—permission to attend a party at a neighboring plantation, a choice piece of hand-me-down clothes—timing his master's level of tolerance so that he would crack at the right moment. And the master would be relieved to have the begging stop and gratified with himself for the affection he engendered among his people.

Ingratiation need not, however, mean mere sycophancy. A servant in a position close to the master could manage to exploit his skills so as to make the master feel dependent. Such slaves would have an area of dominion—the cook's kitchen, the master's or mistress's personal effects and toilet, skills of various learned crafts that were essential to the plantation, sometimes even the management of other slaves. It might start small, but under the right circumstances a wily slave could expand his ground, bit by bit. In time, he could have influence over a wide area of the master's personal and business life.

One treated white people in a strange contradictory manner. They were supposedly wise, powerful, superior: one could not presume openly to be their equal. On the other hand, white people were obviously children, helpless in everyday matters of dressing and caring for themselves or making minor decisions. By reinforcing the notion that petty matters were beneath a master's attention, slaves could gain significant control over that master's day-to-day activities under certain circumstances, nurturing his dependence on them to dress him, keep his life orderly, and remind him of his duties.

The weaknesses that plagued the master—whisky, women, gambling—were the special knowledge of his servants who would accompany him on his rounds and

take him home, often drunk, disconsolate, or broke.
Such frailties were privileged information shared by
both master and servant. The slave might indulge or
encourage the master's habits, or give him mild lectures.
Tortured by guilt over his helplessness, the master might
vent his wrath at his servant in the coldness of day. But
the confidences were likely to weld him to his servant.
The black man, in any case, could make use of his
knowledge. He could exact promises from his master at
opportune moments; he could, indeed, create those moments. He could develop the confidential "brotherly"
role to gain great influence and independence.

We often read of slaves being "broken in"; that is to
say, adjusted and subdued to a new place and new tasks.
New masters and mistresses in established households
might also require adjustment and disciplining by experienced domestics. Few young white women could
take over running a household without dependency
upon older servants. An experienced black woman used
to commanding was not to be easily commanded, especially by a newly married girl with her first house to
run. And young white men, too, could be reminded endlessly of their father's good qualities, of how things were
done under the old master, of the privileges to which
the people at the place were accustomed. When there
was a change in management, much improvement could
come under the guise of the way things had always been
done.

In the close, personal relationships of domestics and
their owners, it took time for each to adapt to the other.
There might be friction and uncertainty for years, but
an adept slave could have much to say in defining his
influence over his master. Of course, masters sometimes
exercised their authority by sending a domestic servant
into the fields or showing a skilled slave his place by

forcing him to do demeaning labor, but most white people wanted a familiar house staff and would suffer arrogance and manipulation to keep it.

While the slave knew the master was the ultimate authority, other whites on the place—wives, older sons and daughters, overseers—had pretensions to power as well. It was thus possible to split these rulers against each other. It was wise to learn who would be most lenient to different kinds of requests so one could get promises the master might feel obliged to honor. Conflicting instructions could provide a ready excuse for failing to do one thing or another. And most families had their own peculiar conflicts: father against son, wife against husband, wife against daughter, sibling rivalries. These could be treacherous waters for slaves, who could easily be caught in cross-currents and suffer from all sides. But such conflicts could also work to their advantage.

When the master did not live on the place, leaving management in the hands of overseers, slaves could sometimes gain leeway. Most masters had little respect for whites who worked for them as overseers, and it was always possible for a cunning slave to play on that thinly disguised contempt. Overseers could be certain that a visit from the master would be the occasion of gossip and tales about his habits as well as those of his wife and children. If he had whipped a slave recently, he could be sure that the master would know. If the overseer was excessively brutal, the master would certainly learn of it, and it might mean his job. It was, nevertheless, a delicate matter, for the master often would talk with great solicitude about his slaves' well-being but do very little to protect them. And once he was gone, the overseer could make the slaves regret having talked against him. But some overseers would work to build good relationships with slaves, hoping to get good work from them as well as good reports to the master.

Vanity was an occupational disease of the master class. To be a proper master meant to be proud. Each could find self-satisfaction in a wide number of things. Some liked their domestic slaves to be elegant and beautiful—to some that meant light skin, to others black; they took pride in the health and strength of their field hands, much as men are proud of prized horses. It showed the master to be discerning in taste, shrewd in collecting, careful and effective in training and discipline. A well-ordered house staff, and good-looking and efficient hands, could make a man feel a master among masters. Some liked to have especially verbal and clever body-servants to travel with. Most took great pride in having musicians to entertain guests and play for dances. Many took great satisfaction in the appearance of scientific efficiency of their plantations.

Slaves were likely to be proud as well. To have one's beauty or strength a mark of a master's pride was gratifying. It was pleasing to serve in what was understood to be high style, to dress in livery, to handle only the finest horses, the best equipment, to be given opportunities in which to be clever. To make music that made others dance, to hear the endless compliments, and to see the pride reflected in the white man's eyes—that too was vanity at work. It explains why slaves preferred a prideful master to one who was middling, having neither class nor style. Of course, the slaves' vanity could serve their masters too. Ironically, the very best slaves were not those who were cowed into it but those whose pride kept them from being less than superior at what they did.

Vanity opened whites to the management of clever

blacks. One need only discover the source of pride. Did the woman think herself pretty? Did she fancy her eyes, her hair, her figure? Did she think herself clever or devastating to men? How easy it was to feed that hunger. Did the white folks think themselves social engines? One could make the parties gay, and there were countless subtle ways to diminish neighbors by comparison. Tell the gentle master how much better he treated his slaves than anyone around, how much his people loved him. Remind him of horror stories of notorious brutes in the neighborhood. Tell the tough man how well he knew his niggers, how much better he was than the soft man who let his slaves run over him. Everyone liked to hear himself praised according to his lights and would be willing to relinquish something for the pleasure of it.

This is not to say that slave con men and women calculated, thus, always precisely and well, nor is it to suggest that white people were such fools that they never suspected soft soap. Some blacks fell so deeply into the act, sensed the thing so intuitively, that after a while it was hardly an act at all. They had become the act. And most whites knew they were being manipulated—how could they not?—but they also believed (or wanted so much to believe) in the source of their pride that they would succumb to flattery even when they saw it for what it was.

Such slave strategies were only open to those who had the master's ear: personal servants, domestics, craftsmen, trusted field hands. The bulk of slaves had no such regular access. Their grievances and hopes to affect the master's will depended upon their ability to persuade the more favored slaves of their cause. They were disturbed by the meanness of an overseer; someone had grievances about intrusions into his family life; an infirm person was given too heavy tasks; such matters could get to the master through those who had his ear.

Such privileged slaves were not necessarily interested in other people's problems, which they might perceive as their own fault. In an abject condition, it is common enough to insist on a distance between oneself and those even further down. Remarkably, however, privileged slaves were, more often than not, intermediaries for their fellows.

There was really no other way within the system. From the outside, the master's authority was almost absolute. From the slave's perspective, it was total. One had either to break out of the system or work within it as best one could. Strategies had to work on the master's personality. Black people always claimed to know their white folks well. It was a necessity.

When black and white people reflected on their experiences together as slave and master, they often used the term "family" to describe the relationship. Such recollections were often sentimental and nostalgic but they did not necessarily suggest a warm and loving family. A feeling of closeness among individuals did not belie the underlying force defining the relationship. Given the fact of coercion, many blacks and whites preferred to emphasize the bonds of sentiment holding them together rather than admit to the reality of power.

It was not contradictory to have familial feelings in a relationship between master and slave. Sometimes black and white individuals spent their entire lives together in the same household. Generations overlapped, so that young and old, black and white, gave to one another whatever sense of continuity was to be had.

The natural rhythms of life punctuated time for all alike. The birth of a child signaled not only new life and a new generation but also, perhaps, the coming to womanhood of a girl whose first cries one also remembered. The marriages of youths—however little black unions were to be honored by whites—marked the time lapse of maturing, raising questions about the wisdom of choice and readiness. Then there was death.

Death made all peer into the chasm. The premature death of youth—the shattering enigma of it, the upward trajectory cut before its zenith—brought all to look into the darkness and ask why. Death in the fullness of one's powers left a void to be filled: at the white man's bier, one's mind searched ahead to the one who would stand in his stead, to the changes that would come. How long would the widow bear her loneliness? What new man would be brought onto the place? What of the future then? Death of the aged left something of the past unremembered. The vivid recollections of the first settlements on the place—those places they had been before, all the people who had come in the beginning and were now gone, dead or sold away. There was in most established households an oral tradition, often sustained by black folk who remembered and never tired of telling of the earliest folk, of remembered Africans with strange ways and words, the generations gone. When such an aged one died, the past was just that much more obscured in darkness.

Such events spoke a raceless tongue. All were drawn for the moment into oneness. All gained, all felt joy, all felt loss in some way. Such living together in a pulsing organism naturally made one have family feelings.

For whites, plantation life was frequently isolated. There would be loneliness even when there were several whites in the family. But often, one or two whites lived for long stretches of time with little company other than

the blacks of their household. Of course, white men on
the larger plantations had many responsibilities that
took them away from home. They took business trips
to the Southern cities. They had to buy and sell, make
arrangements for their business. They were in the government, local or national, and spent much time in one
capital or another. The isolation was especially trying
for white women, who remained on the places, often
managing them, and spinning out their loneliness in
letters and diaries.

The days were long, often hot, and filled with the
place's business. But night fell, suddenly, absolutely
black and silent, except for the sounds of creatures and
the wind. The reliance and dependence of whites on
familiar blacks were crucial in such a world, though
not because of fear that the cabins might send forth
hateful violence to reclaim liberty. That fear was deep
and always present. It was rather the undefinable, inchoate fear of nothingness and meaninglessness and
emptiness that often comes when darkness falls. The
fear of loneliness and isolation has much to do with
identity; we know it best as it first appears in our childhood fears of the dark.

Those who dared to think of it might have nightmare
visions of blacks striking out for some specific or general grievance, slaughtering them all in their beds. There
was slight comfort in knowing that a general rebellion
would surely be put down by the patrols, the militia,
the United States Army, if it came to that, for the white
man or woman might have been engulfed by rage and
hatred before it was put down. There was always security in the knowledge that such occurrences were not
the standard of plantation life. But gossip and news
always carried some item to stir the fear, the uncer-

tainty, that lay dormant in complacency. Things did happen to others, and there was not a white family without its own tales: suspicions of death by poison, arson, sabotage. Such thoughts, like fear of the dark and natural disasters, were part of the condition of life. There was little to do but keep them to oneself.

It was out of such loneliness of fact and fear that some whites drew closer to their servants. These men and women opened themselves in confidence, were generous with affection and fellow feeling, responded to any genuine feeling that seemed to flow back. In such cases, there sometimes grew up a tie of affection deeper than kin—affection and dependency out of one's most secret needs.

It is not surprising that whites held fast to their black "relations," finding in them security, reassurance that theirs was a fellowship based on more than force and unequal gain. The affection whites sought, and often to their satisfaction found, in their servants was to them a testament to their legitimacy and security against dark forces.

It should not be surprising either that some blacks sensing the needs of whites, their hunger for affection and affirmation, responded to those needs and allowed themselves to make their love genuine and warm. One's ability to serve others was gratifying in and of itself, for being a slave carried its own uncertainties and fears. The reciprocal affection that could flow between white and black could give the black servant some special sense of worth, of being loved, of being irreplaceable.

Intimacies came as bodies touched, black skin against white skin. Black women and white women were midwives to one another, pulling life from loins, feeling the other's birth pains as one's own body remembered. The

white infant suckled black nipples, gummed its first
mashed food from black fingers, and rode off to sleep
in the warm, black softness.

Black women and white women nursed one another's
ills over endless nights: wiped sweat from fevered
bodies; listened to cries of pain, the delirium, the whispers of faint survival; cleaned the pus and mucus of
sores and pox; held bodies in their uncontrolled writh-
ings, cleaning away vomit and blood and excrement.
Black hands washed white, still bodies, and shrouded
them into their eternity.

Black bodies and white bodies touched and moved
together in generative acts as well. These were unequal
encounters in which the source of power was never forgotten, but at least individuals did touch one another in
a primal way.

White males were reared to be free sports: they were
expected to sow their oats. While sex with black
women was frowned upon, and any man who had a
reputation for frequenting his slave cabins was likely to
encounter some social ostracism by his white neighbors,
most would admit the Southern white boy found his
first sexual experience with a black woman. Bragging
Southern men asserted it as a fact. But even mature men
were known to have their black children in the cabins.
Masters were tolerant of themselves and their sons, if
not their wives and daughters. Their disapproval of
miscegenation was more likely to fall on overseers and
white interlopers who might threaten the peace of the
quarters.

The nature of the power of master and son was nowhere more evident than in the way the games of sex
could be played. The strategies were simple: get her
away, alone—in a room, the pantry, the barn, an isolated field—some pretext, any order. The game would

begin: first playful, jovial, pleading, and suggestive; then losing patience, becoming direct and commanding. She might plead, laugh, resist, fight him off. But sooner or later it would happen. Perhaps it would be brutal, she falling backward, taking his body onto hers, whimpering and swallowing her hurt. Once it was over, she could walk away ashamed, not because she was prudish or coy, but because her private self had been defiled. This pain would last for a long time to come.

Rape is always the same. But the game was not always so. The young white boy, beyond the first aches of puberty, having played his games of peeping at women in the outhouses, having played with himself despite the pain of it, would be possessed by his fantasies. His lust would be for a grown woman, not a frightened child like himself; a mother, not a sister. In the corners of the kitchen or the rooms of the house, he would pester her while she did her chores. There would be games of teasing and flirting. She played with him; he was such a baby, how he used to trouble her when he was little. Thus, she could prick his soreness. It could be amusing to toy with the white boy and privately pleasing to know someone seemingly helpless ached so much, to dominate youthful dominance. In time, the game would play out, and she would take him to her bosom—or allow herself to be taken—it did not matter. There would be little tenderness to follow. He would walk away as most child-men do, feeling self-satisfied that a mark had been passed to make him a man-child. Yet he would harbor the faint suspicion that he had been mastered, and he might have a slight taste of shame because of that. She might keep the amusement alive for a while, but in time it would fade even if she stayed in the same household or bore the boy's first child.

Black women had little choice in the matter if white men set out to take them. But some might imagine that there was an advantage to their concubinage. Sex too might seem a means of manipulation, a means of giving stability and weight to one's life. It is not a peculiar vanity which assumes that the comfort and love the body gives can make one special in another's eyes. There is a kind of security in the consciousness of one's beauty and the pleasure it gives another. *Where can he find another who is so free with him? He, himself, says that he is free and like another man when he is with me.* The children of her loins were his; they had his looks; they link them together through blood. Was that not an anchor to hold her fast?

It was not strange to imagine that such bonds would assure one's place, would make one's children different from the other black children. It was in its way an escape from slavery, as some few African women had escaped during the middle passage. It was not all in the mind, something she dreamed. Confessions of love were made in the privacy of their lives. She was more beautiful, more warm, than any other woman he had known. She was the only woman to give him real comfort, to understand what he really was and what he really felt. He would care for her, and free her and their children in time. That was the bargain she held to, that generated her life, that was her calculation. Occasionally, she was right.

Beyond the force, the brutalization, the calculated arrangements, we must believe that love of the kind we normally associate with devoted couples did exist. We must believe it because the records tell of it in various ways. The system of slavery and all moral condemnation could not prevent it. Nineteenth-century sexual attitudes and the rather special isolation of Southern white women created an aura of fear and inhibition in sex. White men told themselves so often about the purity of white women and their coldness to passion that hesitancy and foreboding were likely in bed. White women, the nominal equals of their men, were victimized on their pedestal as slaves were on the auction block. They had little power against their men save that of rejection, coldness, and hatred. White women in their beds were one of the only forces in the South that could make white men feel inadequate.

For some white men, the only times in their lives that they were comfortable were with a black woman. For those who had grown up with a black nurse, it had been from the first black flesh—breast, hands, thighs—that had comforted them. It was easy to retreat from a wounding experience into that bosom, always open, always reassuring. White mother and father challenged, made demands, had expectations, were disappointed, set standards according to older brothers, other boys. But the black bosom loved and asked no questions.

Adult white men might well seek the same retreat. For black arms were warm and human. The black body accepted; it did not deny. There he himself could be open. Many white men had such feelings and found in one black woman or another the needed retreat. Many were ashamed and hid from it, and would hide it from the world—selling their woman and her children far from those who would recognize them in their issue.

A few white men, however, faced that reality, found in a particular black woman the love and strength that would allow him to live his life openly in defiance of others, accepted their children as his own, and treated them as his family, as far as the law would permit. Occasionally, such a black woman became the effective head of the household. If there was a white woman, a legal wife, she looked on.

White women had no equivalent sexual outlet. Some, even while complaining of an overseer's or another white man's playing favorites with slave women would draw to their bosoms a small slave child and fondle it as a pet through its youth. Such a pet would always be with her, sleep in her room, be at her feet, a human she could caress who would love her. Too often, however, the rage of white women was vented against their slaves. Should we be surprised to learn that some of the most brutal and sadistic treatment of slaves was at the hands of white women?

Love, affection, and family feeling come through so often in the memoirs of both whites and blacks, yet they always strike the ear as sentimental and false. For what sort of love would support the common practice of giving slaves as gifts to one's children and friends, apparently indifferent to the costs borne by those uprooted? Of course, common sense tells us that people living as masters and slaves would be drawn together by shared human feelings. We do not doubt that or the genuineness of the emotion felt on occasion or even sustained over a lifetime of mutually faithful personal interaction. But the test of love would be if personality could exist outside the rather false insulation of private arrangements. When the trusted and loved slave asked to be free, he often risked being considered ungrateful. The white men and women were few whose love of their slaves would persuade them to face society on their behalf.

The problem was that slavery was a broad social system. While individual relationships might attest to the resiliency of humanity against great odds, even such humanity had to be trimmed and stunted to fit a condition in which one party's humanness could be honored only by the other's will.

When the time came, death ended special arrangements. Wills were read and property was divided up. Perhaps sentimental attachments could continue over the transition. But probably not. Private accommodations were private at last; even heirs could not be expected to indulge "spoiled" servants. And quite often a slave had to be sold away, being property after all.

When all is said, such human interaction was gratifying, but it was possible for only those few blacks who had intimate association with the master's family. Most slaves, those in the quarters, shared little of this. The harsh conditions and economic demands of agriculture determined the boundaries of their lives, unmitigated by the sentiment of white folks.

Thomas Jefferson was known to complain of the uncontrolled rages to which masters were subject. Seemingly rational and balanced men and women strangely fell victim to wild flights of temper, which in their sober moments they would come to regret. Jefferson was not the only white man to note this phenomenon as a characteristic of the master class. It was especially disagreeable to those who would consider themselves polished gentlemen. Some men complained of furies that would make their heads seem to burst and would result in rages against all around them, the lash striking out until the passion abated. Then would follow the remorseful reflection on why they had had such little control over themselves.

Like vanity, rage is an occupational disease of tyrants and despots. Ideally, all was within one's power to command and affect, but reality always proved more complicated. Things rarely occurred the way one would have them: supplies did not arrive when ordered, or they were poor in quality when they did arrive; unseasonable weather forced one to alter plans; people who were supposed to obey did not or did not seem to understand clear orders or carried them out so that the effort was of little use; people who were supposed to be lieutenants gave orders conflicting with one's own. However it was, the will of the master could seldom be translated as he would have it. Such things are frustrating to ordinary men who expect imperfect compliance, but for those whom custom and myth have encouraged to believe in the immensity of their power, such frustrations could be maddening.

The white's experience in America, especially with slaves, led him to be contemptuous of limits. The continent itself, its physical obstacles, fell under the ax of whites and their forced labor. Indian resistance was overcome by cunning and force; nothing could stand in the way of the whites' progress in conquering the land and converting it to profit. Neither were ethics a barrier. Reason could devise convenient excuses for taking Indian land, breaking treaties and agreements, forcing—contrary to all their principals—the labor of black people. Nor did their Christian religion offer meaningful limits. In the Bible, the clever mind could find slavery, or whatever one might wish, explained and justified. Preachers who would make them uncomfortable could easily be replaced by preachers who could make them into God's chosen servants. The laws that they themselves enacted would lighten the weight of government on them, would place minimal and practically unenforceable restraints on their management of slaves, and would remove almost all recourse from those who would think to stand against them.

Masters could do almost anything they liked with their slaves except free them into society. They were not supposed to kill them wantonly, but they could punish them near to death. Even if that threshold were breached and the master had to answer in court, he could assume the court's sympathy in his loss of valuable property and its doubt that as a rational man he would have inflicted such injury on himself with malice aforethought. At his pleasure, he recognized slave marriages and stability of slave families. Approvingly, he presided over slave weddings—sometimes a burlesque meant for his amusement—but he refrained from saying, "What God has joined together, let no man put asunder," for he might do that if it served his needs.

With few physical restraints, and only those ethical ones a tendentious conscience would allow, it was easy for masters and mistresses to assume that it was their right to have unquestioned sway over their property: their lands, their stock, and their slaves. It was almost as if they were God. The blasphemous assumption was not extraordinary. It was vocalized in the master's use of punishment, " to put the fear of God into them." This was standard cant, for slaves were supposed to stand in fear of awesome power. The truth, however, kept coming back in telling failures. They were merely men and women; there were limits, after all. The hubris was enraging.

The Afro-American, especially the slave, had a unique American experience in that he was a creature of narrow boundaries from the beginning. Everything in his life, from birth to death, was to emphasize margins imposed by property and the power of others against him. He was born unfree with no rights vested in him that others were obliged to honor. His future, his potential, the way he would develop his talents, the channels in which they would be employed, were not his to determine. What limited power he could wield came from his precise understanding of these tight constraints and his skills at negotiating them. His life was not a boundless and open sea but narrow, cramped, and treacherous straits through which he would navigate his entire life.

The interplay between master and slave was that between one who saw his powers as practically infinite and one who nurtured his slightest advantage. The slave's sharpest insight into the white character was his perception of its humanity despite its pretensions. White folks might want to think themselves gods but they were humans, and their hubris was an open invitation to a kind of slave power over them.

Some slaves became clowns before their white folks, cavorting, laughing, prancing, doing any ridiculous thing. They would watch the white folks' faces struggling to hold their dignity, their distance, their aplomb, their seriousness. But pushed and prodded, first one then another would burst into uncontrolled laughter. Breathless, the white folks would call their black clown a rascal and send him away; he would be pleased with himself that he had *made* them laugh. They could not resist his power over them.

Some slaves had other techniques. Bright enough to gain the white folks' backing and competent enough to inspire confidence and hope, such a slave would tantalize them with unfulfilled expectations. He would take positions of trust but fall just shy of what was demanded or needed. He would then ride out the storm, feigning dumbness or helplessness in the face of white exasperation. *Send him back to the fields; try him again after he has learned his lesson.* And the game would be repeated until the white folks confessed their fallible judgment or resigned themselves to their belief in the black race's incompetence.

Slaves trying white folks' patience was a standard part of life. Ineptitude, carelessness, clumsiness, forgetfulness, haughtiness, sassiness, insolence, were common words on the white folks' tongues. With such annoying traits, slaves would prod and goad their masters, testing the edges of endurance. They would watch their faces and hear the tones of their rebukes, calculating with finesse the limits of patience. Then the storm would break; and the master, having struggled to maintain calm, control, and mastery, would explode with rage, lashing out at the culprit who was nearest at hand. Finally, the storm would subside, the master remorseful, perhaps, only to be provoked again by someone else. Masters complained often of being taunted by their slaves.

In such perverse ways, slaves managed to gain an upper hand for the moment. The master could be pulled down from his pretensions, reduced to the mere mortal he was. The more he tried to hold himself aloof, be reasonable and rational, the more he tried to hold himself in control—the more vulnerable he became. Despite the pain of a beating, the slaves took pleasure in this kind of control over the master's emotions.

The slaves' consciousness of limitations went beyond institutional and legal definitions or the monopoly of power and violence in white men's hands. Their peasant past and their continued work in agriculture held them to the constraints imposed by nature. They were in touch with the soil, the seeds, the plants; with the boundaries imposed by natural forces—rain, cold, insects that could destroy. They were close to mules and horses, each with its individual spirit and personality, strengths and weaknesses—like all living creatures.

They watched with dispassionate eyes the cycles of life flow through the fields on which they labored, as such cycles commanded their own bodies and those of white folks too.

Their intimacy with nature made them one with the forces of life, which ebbed and flowed, not in the service of people but according to life's own rhythms. It was sobering and humbling to be constantly aware of a largeness beyond oneself, including oneself but stretching into the unknown vastness of time and space. Unlike white folks, who would defy that power, who would identify their will with that of God, black folks natural-istically, almost fatalistically, saw themselves as subject to energy beyond their powers to master.

Black folks possessed a strong sense of the mystical —perhaps an African legacy—which sought identity between thing and spirit, subject and object. Mystery was its own reward; discovering the true mystery was more satisfying than pretentious knowing. They did not expect their minds to comprehend all and did not blame themselves for what they could not understand. They were comfortable with the enigma.

In their eyes, white folks were an awesome but strangely pathetic people. While they were often pious in their Christianity, they had faith only in what their minds and their power could control. They would defy nature and the reasons of life itself if they thought they might profit from the enterprise. Audacity and force had their rewards, but the cost was great in spiritual uncertainty.

As black people looked on, they were impressed by the power of whites, it is true, but they also saw the rest. They saw the dreams of whites to accumulate and be-queath great wealth undermined by vagaries: short-lived sons or those too weak or incompetent to rule;

failure of a distant market to sustain expectations; failures of home and family, health and mind. Slaves' eyes
watched the powerful and self-important wither and die
like other people—sometimes their minds raging into
insanity, sometimes their pride reduced by pain. Slaves
well knew that whatever white men thought of themselves, life and the grave at the end of life reduced all
to the human level.

The mystical mind found metaphysical explanations
in all events. The disasters that came in their time—
crops ruined, accidents cutting off life, poor health—
were signs, warnings, retributions. Nothing, especially
nothing negative, happened without reason. God did
not like ugliness and meanness, and one could always
find in the master's household sufficient cause for any
tragedy. In the eye of the event, there was awe and perhaps sadness but also pleasure in the knowledge that
retribution was in the nature of things, and all would be
resolved in time.

No man or woman is likely to be without hubris: pretensions, pride, aspirations beyond capacity. Slaves had
theirs. But they were people with a strong sense of narrowness of possibilities and with modest aspirations.
The ironies of their lives cut deep, but they were not
dramatic. When they fell on their faces after having
reached too high, the drop was not great. But the
demonstrated frailties of masters were legends to behold. Slaves throughout their days would be moved to
remark, "Oh, how the mighty have fallen!" In this
drama, black people could never lose sight of their own
humanity.

To be a part of a natural universe, a creation that
exceeded human imagining, was a sustaining insight. It
was here that one found meaning in the present and
ultimate meaning as well. It was not just otherworldly—

expecting a better life hereafter—it was existential, being a vision of a moral order against which to measure one's existence, to distinguish between what was and what ought to be. It was a measure against which to judge even the most powerful, to presume a universal force and energy in comparison to which the master's was meager. To be sensitive to one's limits within that order made one indeed more powerful in the end than those who would egocentrically define order in their own terms. White people would reduce God and nature to their own measure in order to understand and enhance themselves. Black people supposed an energy beyond all imagining, power beyond all power, a sense to be felt and not comprehended. Feeling themselves part of that force, they were thereby enhanced.

There was in it something deeply reassuring. That is why black folks held so tightly to their religious expression, why it was never really satisfactory coming through a white ministry. White people always came to remark on it, especially when circumstances shattered their complacency: the apparent placidness and calm assurance of blacks in even the greatest adversity, the strange lack of vindictiveness in most black people. Despite slavery, they seemed as a people to have developed a spiritual base like a rock, appearing sometimes majestic, even aristocratic. It made them the strongest, most enduring force in a changing landscape.

6

The Slave Community

ALL WHO CAME to America were torn from some community. Migration defied those centripetal forces holding the individual in mutual obligation to others. Europeans, pushed by increasingly constricting conditions at home and pulled by the apparently limitless opportunity in America, severed themselves from the nexus of community order. Africans, on the other hand, were rudely snatched from the web that made each of them part of an organic whole. The Americanization process thus weakened conservative and integrating social forces, freeing the individual from community constraints yet isolating him from the power of the community to affirm and sustain him.

Efforts to reassert community ties in America were always problematic, for once personal well-being was given precedence over community and family obligations, the process would be endlessly repeated. For free people in America, it would appear that one's chance was always "just out there," in the next place of development. Roots would never be deep enough not to be pulled up, and each new place would become easier to fit into. Less demanding of commitment, the new place would be abandoned in its turn with few regrets.

In special ways, the same process worked with Africans. Everything in their enslavement in America worked toward the destruction of what remnants of community remained among them. As far as was possible, they were kept away from those of their own tribe or language. As far as was possible, each newcomer was thrown among blacks who had been seasoned in the West Indies or on the Continent. All those social elements that might have made for the re-establishment in America of forms of African community were thwarted from the beginning.

But even after Old World language and culture had been transformed and generations of blacks had created an Afro-American people, both the dynamic character of American life and the peculiar nature of the slave system worked to weaken the possibility of community among blacks. Slavery was, in effect, the removal of black people from the broader commonwealth. Furthermore, slaves were subject to the feebleness of the American community. The weak ties holding their masters to a given place, the fragile white family nexus—the inability of a father to hold his son or daughter to his land and establishment—contributed to the fundamental instability of slave existence. The flux of American life affected them even if they could reap none of the advantages of afforded opportunity.

Furthermore, the rules governing slave life made normal community functions difficult. They could not meet together freely; they could not use drums; there were restrictions against their religious services in cabins or in the woods. Family life was unstable and uncertain. While the master might approve of a family and even give his promise to support it, it could be broken up at a change of his heart or fortune. Indeed, the slave market—symbolic of the general social dynamics—worked to make problematic any permanent establishment for slaves.

Between the conflicting claims of individual and group, community is defined. The enhancement of the one comes at the expense of the other. In general, America has honored self-interest over group interest. But the pursuit of personal happiness was never an Afro-American right, certainly not a right of slaves. Individualism among slaves would have less payoff than among other Americans.

There were some rewards to be sure. Mainly, there was job differentiation and privilege, which depended on the master's recognition of special ability, talent, or responsibility. A slave could benefit by distinguishing himself in the eyes of his master. He could aspire to learn and practice a trade. Working as a craftsman relieved him of tedious and heavy field labor, gave him the personal satisfaction of a skill, allowed him some independence through the chance to earn money, and heightened his sense of worth.

Similarly, there were positions of responsibility, such as driver or overseer. In selecting a black man as an authority over other slaves, the master needed to feel that such a man identified with the master's interests and not with the collective interests of the slaves. Yet, the master might suppose black drivers and overseers could understand, get along with, and manage field workers better than white men. But blacks who did aspire to such responsibility had to distance themselves from other field hands.

House servants, too, chosen and valued for personal characteristics, were considered different from ordinary field slaves. Personal loyalty to the master's family as well as gentility and a polished style were desirable for domestic work. Nowhere was the social separation among slaves greater than between personal body-servants and field hands. The body-servant (valet, personal maid, *et cetera*) was a special breed among the slave population, often commanding an extraordinary fluency of language, a glibness and cleverness attractive in the world beyond the plantation. He traveled with his master: in the country, when the season made that place more agreeable; in the state's capital or Washington, D.C., if his master was in the government; in the North or abroad, if that was his master's style. Such a worldly-wise person could hardly be of one mind with slaves in the quarters.

Striking for freedom was the act of an individualist. Until late in the Civil War, a general emancipation of slaves was hardly conceivable, and collective breaks for freedom were suicidal. Harriet Tubman, Denmark Vesey, and Nat Turner worked for the liberty of all; but most, whatever their sympathy with other slaves, sought freedom for themselves and their families. To purchase freedom or to escape was an act of individuals prepared to break whatever community ties they may have felt with others on their plantation. Only the trusted slave could convince his master to give him freedom by will or purchase; only the audacious could manage a successful escape.

Yet, the individual-versus-group motive was never clear-cut. The choices a master made, consciously or not, promoting slaves from ordinary routine were likely to coincide with the slaves' own consensus. Leadership, after all, developed in the normal work routines in the fields. Some person, for reasons never quite understood, assumed a kind of authority among his peers. It might have been because his voice always started the work songs others would pick up in response, because his voice always called the changes of verse and pace. In such things he could be discernible as one of special character but nevertheless a part of the group.

Slaves conferred other leadership roles on their fellows. Sometimes it was for spiritual qualities—a conjurer or one who seemed to have second sight. Someone of special voice and passion would emerge as a preacher or exhorter. Black men and women developed great authority in the cabins as well as in the master's household.

It is impossible to say where it began. Slaves respected and deferred to those influential with the master, as it was through such people that they would have the ear of the master. But the master risked disharmony if he was unmindful of those who had the respect of the slaves. Choosing a driver, for instance, whose only qualities were strength, loyalty, and the willingness to use the lash in the master's behalf could result in troubled times. But a black man who had some respect among the slaves could get away with being the arm of the master's authority. Thus, it is likely that many so-called privileged slaves were more than self-seeking opportunists.

Privileged status was hard to secure and hard to maintain, requiring tight maneuvering to preserve the master's favor without being isolated from fellow slaves. Some leaned more one way than the other; but to function in the plantation milieu, it was better not to lose the confidence of either the cabins or the big house. Of course, if one was to err, it would be better to lean to the side of the master.

Still, the mark of slavery was not something one "escaped" by upward mobility. One was no less a slave

because one wore livery or nice clothes, spoke with re-
finement, or performed work requiring great skill. It
was not like poverty, a condition one could alleviate by
acquiring money or property. Indeed, one could hardly
escape the *mark* of slavery by becoming free, as slavery
in the United States was a condition of race. If one were
black in a slave state, one was presumed to be a slave.
To be free and black in the South required an explanation. Thus, a free black could never cease having some
identification with slaves no matter how far removed he
might feel himself to be. He might despise blacks and
their condition the more because he was arbitrarily as-
sociated with them. But no achievement or personal
uplift could destroy the primary racial identity. Race,
therefore, forced some element of community sense
among blacks and slaves, whether or not individuals
would will it so.

Individualism of a more destructive kind worked
against the slave community. A system of small rewards
and tyrannical control spawned people who had nihil-
istic contempt for the modest well-being of the quarters.
Cynicism and callowness made fellow slaves the victims
of their frustrated aggression. The strong, sly, conniving,
and ruthless person would appropriate the precious few
things others had acquired for themselves. The chickens,
garden vegetables, and clothes others valued would become his by trickery or bluff. The effort others spent to
gain small margins of comfort for themselves and their
families was erased by those who saw only futility in a
slave's working for his own benefit. At bottom, such
behavior reflected a contempt for self, a contempt for
the slave's condition, and a contempt for all others like
oneself. Why honor the peace and well-being of the
craven and powerless? Why respect the possessions of
those who could not hold onto them? Why respect the

integrity of another's family—his wife, her husband,
their daughter—when such arrangements were feeble
and thrived only by the white man's grace? Deep negation could move one out of fellowship with others,
making them one's prey. Opportunism could become
the single generating value for all actions. Such a person
could be a provocator or an informer with equal ease.

The severing of self from all affectional connections,
the vague sense of mother and father, being traded from
place to place, suffering continually as the victim of
one-sided violence, pushed some into an anomic individualism, which found no sympathy with others and
gave none, which found as much pleasure in others'
pain as in its avoidance. Such a spirit—volatile, unset-
tling, disruptive—would move within the slave quarters,
stealthily, slyly, sometimes with a disarming charm and
wit, but always as a corrupting force. While shrinking
from the white man's power, the disruptive individual
could bluster among blacks. He might urge others into
foolhardy acts while currying favor with whites through
tales of plots and misdeeds. A personality type common
enough among all victims of tyranny, it was undermining to a slave community.

The minds and spirits of some penetrated the mystery and darkness of the nether world; felt the interplay
between spirit and thing; worshiped personal gods;
manipulated the elemental spiritual forces in toads, rep-
tiles, flies, fingernails, pubic hairs, menstrual flow, and
countless, nameless other things that they believed to
affect the living moment. Aspects of African cosmology
persisted in conjuring men and women, born with a
special gift. Conjurers were enigmas in the slave quarters. They drew off to themselves, kept their secrets,
spoke in elliptical phrases—implying worlds, saying
little. Such men and women were sometimes supportive

of community. They were resources who could explain and give meaning to mysterious happenings, and their voices could weigh for the common good.

Sometimes, however, conjurers exploited credulity in such ways as to divide the community against itself. Love potions and charms against evil forces could become instruments of aggression, using the power of the spirit world to gain mastery and control over the wills and interests of others. Pain and misfortune seemed traceable to spells cast by conjurers and called, in turn, for equally powerful spiritual protection. Conjuring, a sometimes benign and unifying influence, could become an evil force, setting black against black, heightening anxieties from justifiable paranoia, and identifying the causes of miseries as preternatural. Such conjurers could stir great distrust among slaves and deflect attention from the true source of unhappiness.

Slaves were powerless to punish or correct "anti-social" elements. The disruptive person was the master's property as much as anyone. This inability to impose sanctions on individuals was a fundamental weakness in the slave community. Lacking power, slaves in the quarters were too often resigned to apathy in dealing with disruptive individuals. Sometimes, of course, collective and subtle sanctions could be effective in isolating troublesome fellows. Group antagonism against anti-social personalities might well account for some chronic runaways. Sometimes, too, the message of inefficiency and disorder would reach the master's ear. If the master could be convinced that his interests would be served in better order in the quarters, he might feed the isolated and disruptive individual into the market.

The slave family, troubled though it was, was the heart of the slave community. The urge to regenerate and to belong to others normally overrode whatever advantages the isolated individual could find. The family fixed the person in a broader nexus, subordinating his interests to those of the group.

The traditional family in Africa extended itself beyond the nuclear group, linking in mutual obligation much of the village itself. It was functional outside the immediate needs of regeneration, conforming to the economic and social realities of production. The obligations of family were related to the survival of all. Dependency was reciprocal: one took from all, and everyone was sustained by one's substance. Individualism and mobility were not valued in such a context. One would think it no advantage at all to be able to move at will, without concern for family or village. While, in modern terms, much was sacrificed for the family and the community, much was gained in one's sense of self and place in the social order.

The New World and slavery were radical breaks in the traditions of black folks. As slaves they were not autonomous and could not make even fundamental decisions about family without the consent of their owners. They had to satisfy the economic needs of others, and their families could exist only as long as they served those needs. Even the responsibility for supporting the family was out of the hands of slave parents. However much they might produce, they could improve the lot of their families only slightly.

According to the conventional wisdom of Europeans, external responsibilities were the civilizing restraints on men and women. Without them, men would be reduced to animals, seeking sexual gratification where they could, unburdened by the need to feed their children; sex partners would be changed freely, without remorse; and children would be abandoned after the first biological necessities of nursing had passed. Most white Americans looked upon slavery as such a state of anarchy and, perhaps fancying what *they* would do without responsibilities, imagined slave families and sexual practices as being closer to those of animals than civilized humans.

Slaveholders persuaded themselves that regular families existed among slaves only because of white tutelage and support. Perhaps they insisted on this view because the obvious weaknesses of the slave's family were due to the pressures of the masters. Even abolitionists tended to view the family life of slaves on plantations as fictive, their sex life as orgiastic in an atmosphere of moral degradation. Neither defenders nor critics of slavery acknowledged the slave's own role in stabilizing family relations.

Such views, however, were self-serving or ignorant. Slaves despite obstacles, managed to build family structures and honor them wherever conditions made it possible. They maintained a strong sense of bond to kinfolk, even those distanced by death or by sale to other parts of the country. They remembered grandparents and parents, brothers and sisters, uncles and aunts, in the names they chose for their children. They did not mimic white families in this nor in their moral attitudes about sex. Blacks adhered with remarkable consistency, for instance, to taboos against marrying with cousins whereas that was a common practice among Southern whites.

There were reasons enough for slaves to want to hold on to their families. The slave had to resist the forces within the system that would isolate him from the community of others, would make him a unit of labor and a commodity in the market. Against the atomizing features of slavery was the possibility of being intimately

tied to other human beings, of seeing oneself projected
and extended in one's children, of passing on to them
what one had learned. Against the pressures of anomie
—of selflessness—one could define oneself in terms of
others who knew all one's strengths and weaknesses,
who gave one affirmation and support. Such hungers
remained even when all the social and economic under-
pinnings that sustained the family had been removed.

All of the American experience tended to split the
individual from the group. The ties of the American
family were generally loose compared with those of the
Old World of Africa or Europe, where the father, because he held whatever resources were available to the
family, expected to manage the lives and marriages of
his offspring. His children responded to these ties and
their dependency by obedience and closeness to the
family. But in the New World, the white father had this
power reduced and the slave parent lost it altogether.
For both, in different ways, family ties were changed
from those of economic dependency to those of affection or psychological needs.

The great difference between the black slave family
and the white family was the nature of the forces working to atomize them. For the white family, there was at
least the illusion of opportunity and change to attract
young people away from the bosom of the family. In
time, it became the American way for youth to strike
out on its own, seeking its own chance. Although this
break often was a bitter one, it was, nevertheless, always
thought of in positive terms.

What pulled at the slave family, on the other hand,
were forces external to its needs and interests. The slave
youth who was sold away was not searching for his own
opportunity. Breakups were only threats to family unity,
nothing more, and they made the slave family defensive

and protective. The frailty of family was only a reminder of the slave's powerlessness and the system's
cruelty. If anything, the idea of family stability gained a
greater importance among slaves than among whites.
To be able to marry, have normal and stable family relations, and enjoy one's children until their maturity
became for blacks a central symbol of freedom, good
order, and the quality of life.

They wanted their marriages to be sanctified and elevated from ordinary life by ritual and ceremony. They
designed such fetes, sometimes with the sponsorship
and cooperation of the master's family, sometimes not.
When most generous, masters offered extra food and
drink for the feast, helped provide bride and groom with
special clothing for the occasion, opened the big house
for the ceremony, and heard the vows themselves. Sometimes the weddings were less splendid, with a black
preacher presiding in the quarters; sometimes the couple
merely did the act common to slave marriages—jump-
ing over a broom before witnesses. Elaborate or simple,
the event was a crucial moment in the slave's life.

Few had illusions that whites perceived these weddings as more than mockeries or amusements. Here was
but another instance in which the master presumed himself to be the only authority powerful enough to give
his consent. Any slave would know that it was different
with white services, where God's blessing was asked.
For slaves, the master's blessing was thought by him to
be enough. The language of the white marriage asserted
that what God had joined no man should sunder. But
the master and slaves knew that such would not be the
case with them: the master had joined them, and he
might rend them as well.

Even when the master approved of the union, the
slave family might be undermined. Much depended

upon the master's willingness to honor commitments. If it was a "broad marriage" and one of the couple lived on a neighbor's place, both owners needed to honor it, allowing the man to make regular visits to his wife. However, slave owners differed in their attitudes toward strong families as a stabilizing force on their plantations. Some were conscientious in attempting to protect slave families, while others were indifferent. A master might interfere in domestic relations if he saw an advantage in doing so. If a man's wife was not fecund, the master might want to pair him with a woman who could produce children. In "broad marriages," the master of the male might grow to resent his neighbor's profiting from the mating by gaining the offspring. The master and his sons or other white men might be interlopers in a slave family, trying to seduce the wife or daughter of a black man. The slave family had little ability to protect itself against whites and had to rely on the master's willingness to assert authority. But even with the most conscientious master, the slave family would not be able to hold together if business required the liquidation of his assets or it suited the creditors of his estate to sever them.

Slaves could hardly hope for the sort of family permanence idealized by whites. Their reality was that partners were likely to be split for sale or hired out at a distance from each other. At a certain age, children became valuable, productive labor in their own right, and might well be sold away. Especially in areas of rapid growth or rapid decline, slave families were victimized by the pressures of the marketplace.

Slave family relations and feelings differed from those of whites, perhaps reflecting traditional attitudes as well as the problems of the institution. Unlike white men, blacks placed no value on virginity in their women, nor did black women who had had previous husbands or partners suffer the rejection of widowhood as white women without property often did.

White attitudes toward purity in women had much to do with male concerns about bloodlines—of knowing one's own son—and the inheritance of property over generations. They had as well deeper psychological roots in an ambivalence about sex and its association with personal sin, weakness, and uncleanliness.

Among slaves there was no shame in finding pleasure in sex. Criticism fell rather on immodesty and flagrant prurience. As in most other things, the sin came not from mankind's inner, personal fault but from outward display and behavior that hurt others and was disruptive to good order. Censure did fall on women who were loose and wanton, who had relations with more than one man at a time. Men, too, who were openly and freely philanderers, taking no responsibility for their offspring, would feel the sting of general displeasure.

The morality that slaves attached to sexual behavior had little to do with what whites would consider purity. Slave parents could carefully discipline and protect their daughters from encounters that might lead to careless sexual liaisons, but no obloquy attended a girl merely because she became pregnant without being formally attached in marriage. She was most likely to be accepted as wife of her lover or, if not him, another man who would accept her child as well.

Black women were a protected class in neither myth nor reality. They were working, productive labor. They worked beside their men, doing nearly all that men were expected to do. There was no presumption that they were fragile. Their backs were bared and they were beaten raw as were the men; their being with child seldom mattered. They were stripped and examined in

slave markets as were men, with little deference to their
modesty. They were given no quarter except for brief
periods ending their pregnancy and following their de-
livery of a child. Even then, many were forced to work
against health's interests.

Most often, the division of labor gave women more
work than men, for they were required to prepare meals
in the evenings, clean cabins, and keep clothes in repair.
While their husbands had their own chores and would
help them, theirs was a long and hard day. Although
most of the roles of leadership were male, there was
little of the male dominance in the slave cabins that
characterized the white household. Nonetheless, women
honored their men.

Women, of course, were tied to young children, but
sales of children in their early teens could sever mother
from child. Even so, mothers had a greater chance of
remaining with children than did fathers. Some fathers,
however, made superhuman efforts to reach their children and families in distant places.

Black males, like whites, found personal pleasure in
looking on their children, but their affection tended not
to be exclusive or protective. There was with them no
problem of legitimacy in inheritance, since they had no
property to pass on to their children. One could feel
himself the "father" of any man's children as well as his
own. A craftsman would likely take a child often not
his own under his wing. A man who could fish or set
traps for animals would likely have a child on his excur-
sions. No children on a plantation were without adult
figures—male and female—who would teach them and
discipline them and show them love.

Children came hard because of high mortality, and
those who survived were the more precious because of
it. After a brief convalescence, the mother returned to

the fields, while the child would begin life on the large plantation in a communal fashion. The nursery might have several infants under the care of an old woman or man who was too feeble for other work. As soon as they toddled, the children were taken in charge by other children, who acted as their nurses and teachers.

Much of their first language derived from games endemic to a childhood society: rhythm-and-rhyme games, running-and-hiding games. Education came naturally from such games and from chores of gradually increasing arduousness and responsibility. Roughly, the children matured in age-grade patterns. Those eight to twelve years of age had charge of the smaller children and did light chores. From twelve to fourteen, children had heavier chores—carrying wood and water, helping in the kitchen, working in the family gardens, cleaning the cabins. From fourteen to sixteen, chores became heavier, productive labor; by fifteen, most children were in the fields. In addition, by this age, slave children had learned the work routines of the place. Adult slaves drew the children into sewing, basket weaving, carving, hunting, fishing, and other skills.

The day-to-day life of the slave child held important lessons about the limits of his world. The white world and the black world were joined on the place but were, nevertheless, separate—big house from cabin, power from powerlessness. The white children and the black children were playmates and shared much early education. But white children were soon to adopt the roles of little "massa" and little "missus." The playfulness and affection as well as the cruelty of children emerged in the one-sidedness of white over black. In time, the white children went away to school or had tutors brought onto the plantation. Here was a telling division, for what white children were expected to learn was proscribed to their black playmates.

Some black children would never forget the trauma of that separation; they would forever place a magical significance on the written word and the power of reading. Some slave children were able to snatch bits of the alphabet and phonetics. Perhaps their white playmates gave them their first lessons; perhaps one of the master's family indulged the child as a pet and taught some reading; perhaps a literate slave passed his knowledge on to one child or another. It was a dangerous knowledge to have, and its discovery could incur the wrath of whites.

The slave child had to learn the most essential lessons of racial etiquette, to know the reality of all earthly power being in the hands of others. The child had to learn to take pain and absorb it. To fight against pain and humiliation could mean disaster; and no black person, neither mother nor father nor sister nor brother, could be of help. None could protect the person against the lash; none could protect himself. None could even shield his eyes from the view of loved ones being whipped, brutalized, killed, or sold away. To prepare against such pain was to inflict pain. So father and mother never spared the rod against their children. They inflicted pain (the pain they themselves had borne), for their children had to know their limits and had to know the lash throughout their lives. "To stay in line" was to reduce the incidence of punishment; that would be the parents' greatest hope. The pain of the lash was the shared experience of slaves. The family felt for one another, and all slaves were touched by it the same.

The lessons of the limits and bounds that power imposed on the slave were coupled with instructions as

to how to manage white people. The unerring sense of
vanity and human weaknesses would become instinct.
How must one play on them? The right tone of voice to
get what one wanted or to avoid punishment; the way to
make one's inferior status work to one's interests—the
mask of dumbness, of helplessness, would be studiously
acquired. But there were other styles—weapons, if you
will—sharpness, sarcasm, sly and cutting ways, impu-
dence. One learned to walk a tight line that tempted
punishment but avoided it for the most part. Some slave
children learned from their grownups that white people
could be played like instruments—some of them became accomplished at it.

Childhood was a common school in survival without
power. It was no trick merely to stay alive: any animal
could do that. The art was to learn to manage a narrow
situation, where pain was often one's lot, and pull from
it something of personal pleasure—something good to
eat, a splash of color to wear, the joy in one's body, the
delight of dance and music, the ability to find love in
another and to create space in which the personal self
could exist and breathe. These were the most important
lessons for the slave child to learn. They were crucial
to his survival and to his sanity. Any black growing up
on a plantation could find in black men and women this
self-same intelligence.

The odds were not good that the slave family—father,
mother, and children—would hold together. Threat and
uncertainty made the slave's family even more meaningful. Blood relations and kin were bases of real affection
and obligation. During slavery, men traveled long distances during holidays to be with family. After emancipation, the motive force of most freedmen was to find
mother, father, brothers, sisters, wife, husband, and
children.

Almost any slave quarters, then, had children and older people who were separated from kin who were somewhere else or dead. But the life of the quarters worked against isolation. Unattached children were assimilated into other families as a matter of course; and old people, too, were drawn into some circle, that they not be isolated. In this way, family extended beyond blood and was inclusive of those in need of protection.

Thus slaves in their quarters worked against those forces that would atomize them, that would pull the individual out of the web that gave each meaning. Although the rending of their lives and personal associations was to be commonplace, all of their instincts were to knit over the rupture, to bring the isolated and abandoned person into a collective "family" network.

In the evening hours following the supper meal, the family found itself gathered around the cabins. Fires glowed into the night as men and women sat and smoked their pipes and told stories. The children heard of rabbits, bears, and foxes; stories of times before they were born, of where the folks were before coming to this place, of strange black men who hid in the forests and swamps raiding white people's storehouses for their food; and they heard of old men and women who spoke in another tongue and who came from Africa, where all their folks before them had been and where one could do as he pleased. The fires and the stories drew the quarters together in the night.

In those Africans who first professed Christianity and mimicked the European's style and language, there was a seeming surrender. It appeared to be an abandoning of the faith of their ancestors, the giving of themselves over to the deities of their masters. It seemed to sever what possible unity there could be among the captive black people, for like acquiring European techniques, Christian conversion was a means of distinguishing oneself from other slaves; it was a means of placing a distance between oneself and others, of despising the "pagan" ways and becoming one with white folks. In the seventeenth and eighteenth centuries, black converts to Christianity were often derided by those who clung to African ways or resisted surrendering their spirits to white folks' ways. However, by the nineteenth century, most slaves could be said to be Christian of some sort, and that minority which clung to beliefs and practices reminiscent of Africa was thought by blacks to be strange and exotic. At the time of the Civil War, the Afro-American people were a Christian people, almost entirely Protestant, following Methodist and Baptist ways.

Yet the conversion process had been problematic from both the black and the white point of view. Whites were never comfortable with the idea of their slaves being drawn into Christianity. They never lost the suspicion that there was something subversive to slavery in the doctrine that all men were worthy before God; they sensed a basic contradiction in both masters and slaves being part of a Christian fellowship; and at the very bottom, for those only slightly thoughtful in their faith, there was the gnawing certainty that one could not be a Christian in God's eyes and do what one needed to do to run an efficient plantation. Moreover, many slaveholders felt that religious meetings among slaves could be converted into conspiracies, that preachers and exhorters could too easily become provocators, and that the emotional excesses of slaves' worship could incite disorder.

What slave Christianity there was, slaveholders wanted to control. They would prefer to have white preachers instruct slaves because their Christian doctrine was orthodox with respect to slavery and their social message was agreeable. They would try to prohibit black preachers, fitfully most of the time but stringently after an event like the Nat Turner insurrection reminded them of potential dangers.

Oddly though, the process of Christianizing the Afro-American was not one of abject surrender of Africa to the West. In the spirit of Afro-Americans, Christianity was converted to their needs as much as they were converted to its doctrine. So, while conversions could be divisive among blacks, in time the Afro-American world would utilize Christianity in such a distinctive way as to give itself its own integrity. Their religion would be their principal defense against the multiple attacks on the slave personality, and it would be the chief means of community among slaves, comprising shared experiences and shared values.

The white ministry that served slaves was sometimes genuinely committed to saving their souls, but most often the master whom those ministers served was of this world. Clergy who were critical of slavery or presumed to judge the practices of slaveholders had become quite rare by the mid-nineteenth century. The others preached a gospel of obedience of slaves to masters, told slaves to expect a reward after death, and heaped upon them the guilt for any disorder: stealing, lying, cheating, laziness. They were the instruments of a master class attempting to appropriate the slaves' natural religious sensibilities for their own uses.

Slaves opened themselves to the message of Christ. They sat in the balconies or in the back pews of their master's church. They listened respectfully to the preachings of the white men brought onto the plantation by their master, just as they listened with due respect to their master's own versions of the Christian message. But none of this was their religion. It spoke out of the same Bible they called Gospel, and it used the same symbols and metaphors; but when the slaves thought of their religion, they meant that worship with black preachers or exhorters they knew in their cabins or in the woods at night. More precisely, they meant that worship they were forced to keep secret from their masters and the slave patrols.

It was obvious to the most credulous among the slaves than their master's gospel was self-serving, meant to rationalize and justify their enslavement. Even in its best voice, it did not speak to the spiritual needs of slaves. However eloquently spoken, it came from the spiritual needs of the oppressor to the ears of the oppressed, who hungered to find their meaning for themselves, reassuring them in their humanity.

However, the Christian message did speak to the slaves' condition. It told Old Testament tales of Hebrew children enslaved and oppressed; of Moses, the deliverer, who led the people out of oppression; of a tribal deity who protected a righteous people; of prophets and exhorters who excoriated against all pervasive evil, pointing the way to unity with the Mind and Soul of the Father; of a personal God who would deliver Daniel from the lion's den, Jonah from the body of a whale. The Father was the Lord and Soul of creation, at once authority and source of personal and individual spirit.

The story of Christ told of the ultimate sacrifice, the love that encompassed all, included all. Deep in Christ's story lay the birth of the lowly, the apparently insignificant person, who was, nevertheless, the Son of God: "An' they didn' know who He was." It was the story of Christ the innocent, the helpless, the child of Mary, the Lamb of God; Christ the friend of the meek and the humble; Christ the scourge of the moneychangers in the temple, the confounder of those who would twist the teachings of God to serve selfish ends. In that story was the suffering of the powerless and the betrayed—pain was the sign of righteousness. It was also a story in which the big man was reduced and the little man uplifted.

Christian legends were an endless resource for the slaves to draw on, in which to find their experience explained. There was a wealth of symbols that evoked emotional links between the slaves' reality and a spiritual tradition. There was the style in metaphor, analogy, and parable, which served the slaves' purpose—to communicate felt understandings to one another.

The slaves withdrew from the white man's presence to find their religious selves—at best it was in their cabins or in the wooded hollows of the neighborhood. The meetings merged the "word" from the Bible—in the mouth of the black preacher, in the people's sounded responses, songs, and dancelike shouts. It was not one thing alone—the words of the preacher or the sound and movement of the people—but a wholeness, an atmosphere in which the spirit lived and the soul moved. Black worshipers wanted to create that atmosphere so that the spirit would live among them.

Black preachers developed a style that neatly fitted the needs of their people. Their service fell into an almost ritualized pattern. They would begin with a text: a story from the Bible, something Jesus or Moses said or did, a question about the nature of God's or man's predicament. In the first phase, the preacher spelled out the story, explored its most obvious meanings. His pace would be moderate, his language visual, perhaps developing a dominant metaphor around which he would build his message, and he would at intervals call upon his people, and they would respond: "Is that right?" "That's right. Amen, Lord!" "But you know that." "Yes, that's right, Lord!" And he would urge them on: "Am I talkin' to myself, Lord?" "But nobody's prayin' with me."

He would move into a second phase without mark, weaving in the specific, everyday reality of the worshipers. His phrases would be quicker, more intense; he would repeat himself in shorter and shorter cadences, gasping at the end, slapping his hands. As the rhythm quickened, the worshipers' responses came more quickly, too; and people's voices could be heard fully repeating his phrases. At a crest of intensity, when the world of the here and now and everyone's reality had been meshed with the world of Jesus—the holy world —he would shift into intense words directly with the Lord. He would talk to the Lord as an intimate. The people, riding on the crest of his excitement, one and then another, would be drawn upward, shouting and trembling with the evoked spirit commanding the body and the voice. And it would go on until the unison of voices—the preacher's and the worshipers—subsided into slower, breathed cadences, calling softly to the Lord. Then a voice would pick up a song, and first one, then another would take up the song until all were singing, the still-electric atmosphere slowly losing its charge in spent emotion.

The style of the black preacher was universal because it was the product of a mass experience. The congregation gave the emotional setting for the religious response; the preacher served and inspired that community experience. He did not create it. While there was a formula, congregations did not respond to all who were preachers. There was the contriver who would pull out all the stops, conscious of his tricks and devices, some part of him remaining detached, outside the event. Others bore through to their nerve endings, exposing and opening themselves so that the spirit might flow, freeing everyone of pretense and guardedness. Some men had a gift to quicken the spirit in everyone, and black folks understood that such a gift came to otherwise ordinary men. They were not surprised to see in their preachers the human faults and weaknesses of others. It was not contradictory, because they were not holy men. Like everyone else, the preacher had to be forgiven his foibles; but in the scene of worship, when he was possessed by his God, he must be sensed honest.

The congregation was the basis of black religion. Little in black religion was geared to the isolated individual. While meditation and prayer might be private, one expected to come closer to the spirit in the congregation. Because there was little emphasis on personal guilt, there was never a strong ascetic spirit. Being by all standards the lowest of the social order, with no glut of worldly goods or materialism, slaves felt no need to be mendicants.

Slave worship was a group phenomenon because the group provided the context and the ambience in which the internal spirit could be let out, the external spirit let in. In this way the object of slaves' worship was realized: to re-establish the relationship of self with the life force of the universe; to achieve unity of the self with all life.

Black religion was thus a celebration of life, of feeling, of both the tangible and the spiritual. The great joy was in the reaffirmation by the living spirit that the self was part of the living substance of all life, and that one had meaning, therefore, in the largeness of life, the bosom of God. This was a guarantee of support in this world as well as in the next.

In this community experience was verification that what was felt was real, that when one said, "I am the child of God," there was assent without question—there was "Amen." All shared the experience and the feeling; there was a drawing together. The quarters' shared anxieties—changes in the management of the place, threatened sales, a new overseer—could be released in group worship. The black driver at odds with fellow slaves because of his role could be drawn into fellowship once again in worship.

The pain brought down on one person—the lash drawn across one's back until the blood came, salt rubbed into the wounds, fellow slaves made to watch mutely—could be followed by a stealing away together into the woods. There voices would together supplicate God to heal the pain of a brother or sister, a pain that all had borne, that all were likely to bear again. In the evocation of that shared pain, all would find a remnant joy in one another and in the faith shared by each, sustained by each. The body's wounds ached still, but the soul was embraced in the collective soul, where there could be peace.

The tyranny of slavery left the slaves in jeopardy of losing themselves—as they would see it, of losing their souls; or, as we might see it, of the disintegration of their personalities and the loss of their integrity. That was the greatest danger. The threat derived from the very fact of unmitigated oppression and the total subjugation under which slaves existed. As a people, they had been snatched from a place where they belonged and thrust into a new world where they were forced to labor—despised and rejected from ordinary community involvement, commanded and limited in all aspects of their lives so that normal matters of birth, family, and death were at the disposal of others. Given this experience, they might have been described as victims of those of greater power. Had they been just victims, though, the story of the Afro-American would have been a different one. Somehow they managed, even as slaves, to transcend the role of victim and to take their souls into their own hands. This was their superb genius and their ultimate heroism.

As oppressed people, their souls' great challenges were three: that they might fall victim to fear of their oppressor, that they might compromise integrity by deception, and that they might give over their souls to hatred—natural enough tendencies given the circumstances. Some slaves succumbed to them, but the remarkable thing is that most did not.

For the victim of oppression, fear, craven and unabashed, where the heart leaps always in the throat, was the first danger. Better to shrink away into oneself; dare not take wife or husband or give love to anyone, because only deep hurt could follow. Fear pulled one back. One might cower before the white man or grin always, converting oneself into a bowing sycophant in order that one be neither hurt nor destroyed.

The second hazard was duplicity. Weakness seeks compensation for its impotence. Although powerless, the slave could see weakness and blind spots in the powerful and play games of deception to manipulate him. He is a vain fool like other men, more so because of his power. So why not find the mask that is most congenial to him, wear it to his pleasure and one's own profit?

The mask, however, is a threat to the soul, because it converts the lie into a style of life, a method of survival. One cannot wear the mask to deceive without the mask becoming oneself in some way. White folks loved to see the darkies clown, liked to think that they were children, burlesques of normal human life. Some blacks played that role—wore the sambo mask—to smooth their way. As long as they were fully conscious of the game, they could laugh at the deception, at how easily they could put on "ole massa." But the danger was that the lie became real as, in time, they converted themselves to the service of white folks' egos. Then, the genuine self would be lost beneath the mask.

The third peril was to fall victim to hatred. One could be driven into a corner where one's only choice lay between humiliation and physical pain. One could find one's strength and will insufficient against the great odds of men and machines and weapons, or stand by and watch, or suffer in one's own body the rape by ugly power. Under such conditions the soul turns inward and outward to exorcise the bitter reality of impotence. Searing hatred that is turned inward on the self and its powerlessness, and burning singleminded hatred turned outward on the oppressor focus all one's being on the single release, the destruction of self, perhaps through striking a blow at the victimizer.

Fear, deception, and hatred endangered the slave personality because each placed his entire being at the disposal of his oppressor. The view of reality narrowed down to the white man—the master class—his will, his judgment, his behavior. Whatever the master did, whether it be conscious or not, became the generative force guiding the victim's reactions. Whether through fear, trickery, or hatred, the victim would define himself in terms of the master's will.

For many, the slaves' religion was their protection against such character disintegration, for it placed them in an ethical order that transcended both them and their oppressors. It provided a perspective from which to look on themselves and white men, and to find a way of measuring and judging. Indeed, their religion obliged them to judge.

No matter how justified the fear, how genuinely helpless they were, in their view they were in God's hands. It was not just a fatalism but a sense of protection and a sense of home. They were a part of the natural universe, which awoke with color and brilliance in the day, broke the rivers into millions of diamonds in the sun, flowered and fruited and childrened everywhere. Their bodies and their hearts affirmed that oneness with fish and birds and God. Their songs would say, "I got a home in that rock, don't you see"; and in an ultimate way, fear could be managed with such a view, leaving deception and hatred behind.

Religion insisted on a truth and standard for all humankind. God did not make a person to be a clown. There was presumed to be a standard of dignity to which creation called a person to hold himself, obliging him to be honest; and it provided the Christian slave, confronting his Christian master, with techniques that could undermine the master's power over him.

The slave's religion protected him against destructive hatred by underscoring in himself his sense of worth. As long as he could believe himself worthy in God's eyes, he was guarded from self-contempt, which is the other side of hatred.

It was indeed these qualities among slaves that enabled them to survive with integrity; and it was these qualities that caused whites, looking on or as agents of oppression, to remark at the strength and natural dignity of black people. It was also these qualities that made it possible to create a slave community.

7

Nominal Freedom

IT MIGHT HAVE BEEN that the society, caught in an ironic and tragic circumstance, found itself burdened by laws and an institution from which it could not be extricated. A weak and irresolute people might well have been unable to realize their ideal of building a free society without intentional and purposive exploitation and oppression. There would be slaves, alas, and there would be free people. One day, someday, the one would be incorporated into the other, and there could be social integrity and harmony. That was not the case, of course; and by mid-century hardly any white Southerner could be found to think ill of their peculiar institution and few white Northerners were prepared to face courageously the social consequences of an America in which slavery was abolished. The true measure of their joint complicity in tyranny was not the fact that they lived with slavery but the conditions they imposed on those black men and women who were called free.

From the first awareness of English settlers that their future in America, their prosperity, and growth as a colony would depend upon the labor of Africans in large numbers, they were put in a quandary. As adventuresome as they might have been, they were not ready to accept the challenge of creating a new community of peoples from different cultures—European, African, and Native American. Rather, they looked to establish a society that was "civilized," all the while conscious of how delicate and fragile that "civilization" was. The educated among them recognized that it was only in the recent past that they had been drawn into the culture of the West, which they admired. Even so, the "civilizing" qualities of the Continent often seemed merely to be an Englishman's veneer. One did not have to scratch deep to detect a rawness and boorishness, which was missing from the French and Italians, say. They were far too close for comfort to what they saw as the savagery of the Irish and the Scots.

As Englishmen in wilderness outposts, the Southern colonists were not about to relinquish their toehold claims to being "civilized" people. They would be a city on a hill in ways other than that in which the Puritans had conceived it. All the world would judge them by how they resisted the forces that tried to pull them back into the morass of the uncultivated. It had already proved difficult. Men had escaped to live with Indians, preferring that life to one among the whites of the colony. Some had fallen into sexual perversities with animals, and some had turned to cannibalism during times of starvation. The ground that held them above the pit was thin enough without the distinctions between themselves, and black men and red men being lost.

While the courtly class in England could find quaint amusement in the occasional African in someone's retinue and remain indifferent to mulattoes in their midst, the Anglo-Americans had too much at stake. There would be no fascination for them in racially mixed villages, no beauty in the blending of blood. When they looked at themselves, they wanted to see Englishmen, and they wanted others to have no confusion as to who they were. Otherwise they might be seen as freakish oddities, curious examples of what would happen to "civilized" men let loose in a wild country among wild people.

Their quandary was how to preserve such a distinction yet depend upon the labor of imported people, whom they must avoid. The Africans would arrive in large numbers and, in time, would become a substantial part of the settlement. How could they import Africans, profiting from their sale as well as their labor, without converting the new country into settlements like the West Indies and the black tropics, more a New Africa than a New Britain?

Slavery was the solution, for it gave blacks a permanent, lifetime status within a separate racial category. It was a means of pushing them into a defined social context, elemental to the general social and economic fabric but apart from it. This development foreshadowed the Afro-American condition: servile, and in the lowest social position but different from a low social class in that no objective circumstance—neither skill nor dress nor education nor manners—could modify the fundamental arrangement. It was a racial accommodation whereby the white community would be dependent upon the black population, and blacks would be a caste apart.

Ideally, all whites would be free and all blacks would be slaves. If white planters had realized their utopia, they would have created a community of free white men served by an army of black servants. If whites failed to achieve great wealth, were modest, poor, or unable to command blacks to their advantage, they were free nonetheless. If blacks managed to acquire the trappings of culture—religion, knowledge, skills, or modest personal property—they remained enslaved and alienated. White and free, black and slave: it would have been a simple, unambiguous matter.

But utopias are really nowhere; and the realities that came to pass in the new country made for many ambiguities. From the beginning there were those who did not fit: blacks who were somehow without white masters and were, therefore, free men; whites and blacks, males and females, who found lovers in one another and who, in time, gave birth to another kind of anomaly—the person of mixed blood, who would be indistinguishable from white folks. Thus, in the real world, "white" people could be slaves and black people could be without masters. It would perplex American society at least until slavery ended.

From 1619 until the 1660s, when laws defining Africans as slaves signaled the direction and intent of Virginia and Maryland, those few Africans and West Indian blacks who happened to arrive had an uncertain status. Many whites who purchased them by paying the cost of their transport assumed that they were like other indentured servants: they would be obliged to service for a stipulated period of time and then be freed. Even after the passing of laws defining a slave status for blacks, some masters continued to give black servants their freedom after they had served an "indenture."

A small number of blacks gained their freedom during the colonial period as a result of the conviction held by some that Africans could not be enslaved once they had professed their Christianity. More often, Afro-Americans who gained their freedom did so as a reward for special service to their master, such as being an in-

formant about the crimes or plots of other blacks. It
was the master's form of gratitude. Others won their
freedom by serving the colony in a meritorious way—
in Indian wars, perhaps.

Some children of black men and white women were
able to win their freedom in time because of the stipu-
lation that children should follow their mother's condition. Often a white man's concubine and their children
were freed as a sign of his remorse or affection. Along
the Gulf Coast, which had long been under the rule of
the Spanish and French, there was a notable population of free persons of color who were the offspring of
European fathers and black mothers. Many such fathers
treated their mulatto children as legitimate, educating
them in European schools and bequeathing to them
property and sometimes slaves. Such men and women
were people of influence and wealth.

By the Revolution, there was a small number of free
blacks in the Anglo-American colonies, but the oddity
of their position was strongly felt: most of the colonies
had passed laws prohibiting the manumission of slaves
in the 1730s. Those few who had managed a nominal
freedom despite the laws owed their fortune to the protection of their white fathers.

The Revolution threw much into disarray. With their
masters at war and with the promise of freedom for
those who were able to escape to the British, many
slaves took whatever opportunities they could find to
get to the British side. Slaves stole themselves and their
masters' horses and guns to join Lord John Murray
Dunmore off the coast of Virginia; some participated in
raids against the colonists. On the other hand, slaves
served a colonial army that was more than reluctant to
accept them. Generally, such service would result in
their freedom.

Although some of those who joined with the British were resold into slavery in the West Indies, many held on to their freedom in Canada or Africa; they were, thus, removed from the stream of American slavery. Those who gained their freedom serving in the Continental Army were the beginning of a wave of newly freed blacks who appeared in the wake of the Revolution.

Several forces combined to spur the manumission of slaves in the years following the war. Many of the colonists were infected by the revolutionary ideology and rhetoric to the point of sensing that blacks as well as whites had a right to liberty. Embarrassed by the inconsistencies of slavery in a nation founded on the principles of individual liberty, they successfully brought pressure to repeal the Maryland and Virginia laws prohibiting manumission. Masters were then free to act on their conscience.

The economic depression following the Revolution brought with it misgivings about the future of the Southern economy. This was especially true as the South, no longer a part of the British mercantile system, lost the subsidies supporting its products in the English market. Southern tobacco, for instance, now had to compete in the world market without British price supports. There was good reason to suppose through the first decade of the nineteenth century that the old tobacco culture was dead in the Upper South, and Virginia and Maryland would be hard pressed to find other means of prosperity. This economic weakness encouraged the belief that whatever the ethical problems of slavery, it would become an economic burden to planters. There might even come a time when planters would not be able to sell the products of the slaves' labor at a price sufficient to feed, clothe, and house them. Many masters wanted to be freed from slavery so that they could have wider options for investment and wealth.

Probably, had someone devised an operable scheme that would have compensated slaveholders for the loss of their slave property or had there been some conversion of their capital investment in slaves into some other form, and had there been some plan whereby all those of African descent could have been removed from the society and from the path of American expansion, slavery would have ended in Delaware, Maryland, and Virginia just as it had in the Northern states. Many talked of compensation and the impossibility of a mixed society, but nothing came of it.

In the meantime, many masters freed some of their slaves. Some, like George Washington, freed nearly all of them, setting them up on land to work. Others freed favorites or took the occasion to liberate blood kin. Blacks took advantage of the liberalized atmosphere, finding ways to purchase their freedom from their owners and, sometimes, that of their families as well. Other blacks found the courts open to suits claiming free status for one of several reasons, such as the discovery in their past of a white, freeborn female forebear. Even in situations where the law was not favorable to manumissions, slaves and their owners learned how to gain de facto freedom while the bondsman remained nominally a slave. For the black person such quasi-slavery had the advantage of avoiding the problem that other free men had of explaining his status. On paper he was a slave and that was all that mattered to a society which would presume freedom to be exclusively a white man's condition. Often, blacks bought persons out of slavery and, for legal convenience, became masters of those they purchased.

Thus, in the Upper South between the 1780s and 1800, there was a rapid growth of the free-black population not only in numbers but also in kind. Whereas before the Revolution, the small free-black population tended to be privileged—children of white fathers, with property and skills—the manumission in the wake of the war was general and benefited a wider range of slaves. Thus, the free-black population of the Upper South became darker in color and included men and women without skills, property, or white protection.

It became increasingly difficult to tell who was who. Formerly one could assume that any Afro-American was a slave, especially if he were dark. Now it was especially confusing, since the many literate people in the free population helped others get some written documents attesting to their freedom. It became easier, therefore, for a slave to escape to a city and pass himself off as a free man, and for a fugitive to find help and shelter or to be helped out of the country.

Those blacks who claimed to have served the Continental Army or their masters in the war, those who benefited from the uneasy conscience of their owners, those who took advantage of changed attitudes by purchasing freedom for themselves and their families, and those who seized the moment to escape made up the swelling population of free blacks. This post-revolutionary growth was smaller in states like South Carolina and Georgia, where revolutionary sentiment was not so effective, where there was a larger proportion of black to white, and where the commitment to slavery was strong.

Immigration also added to the numbers of free blacks. In the wake of the 1795 uprisings in Saint-Dominique, large numbers of immigrant came from the West Indies. Many were mulatto émigrés who had found themselves on the wrong side of the revolution. Despite resistance, they flocked into the Southern port cities of Charleston, Savannah, Mobile, and New Orleans, bringing with them both the anxieties of a violently displaced people and expectations that a social system of three castes—white, black, and mulatto— would continue.

The expansion of this free-black population ended in the first decades of the nineteenth century. Whatever the ambivalence of whites in the Upper South, there developed no way out of their dilemma, no feasible scheme whereby slaveholders could receive compensation for their lost property. The growing number of free blacks only intensified the conviction that there could be no satisfactory biracial accommodation and that blacks would have to be transported elsewhere if slavery were to end.

Early efforts to rid the country of slaves and free blacks at the same time resulted in schemes such as the American Colonization Society, established in 1817. They hoped to persuade slaveholders to manumit slaves who would be deported to a colony in West Africa. For a while the Society received support from treasuries of states in the Upper South. It was headed at various times by James Madison, James Monroe, and John Marshall. Much of the support for the colonization movement was in the interest of removing an unwanted free-black population and not in ending slavery in the United States. By 1860, approximately 15,000 Afro-Americans had been colonized to Liberia, about 12,000 having been transported through the efforts of the American Colonization Society. The great preponderance of these immigrants had been free to begin with; few slaves found freedom this way.

Reasonably enough, blacks deeply distrusted the col-

onization movement and the motives of its leaders.
Furthermore, most blacks, slave and free, felt their
rightful place was in America. This was their native
land. They had an obligation to prove themselves in
this society. It would be immoral to abandon those who
would remain in the country as slaves.

Sufficient numbers of whites knew there was no way
their region could grow and prosper without the labor
of black people. Continued slavery seemed the only
answer; and with the message that the Saint-Dominique
émigrés brought in their baggage—that order was
fragile in a slave society—whites began to retreat
from their revolutionary openness. In time, they came
to feel that slavery and the absolute control of race under slavery was essential for continued well-being, and
they began to view the confusion of racial bifurcation
in the status of free persons of color as a threat to the
logic, if not to the system, of slavery. Some, too, would
claim slavery to be more than a practical accommodation to a difficult situation; it was a positive good.

Economic changes also helped to counter the movement in the Upper South to free slaves. By the 1830s,
cotton culture had expanded in the Deep South and the
Southwest. The expansion of agriculture in Georgia,
Alabama, Mississippi, Louisiana, and Arkansas further
increased the demand for slaves. With the slave trade
having ended in 1808, Upper South planters now found
themselves with a slave property which, far from becoming a burden, had become an asset easily convertible into cash and profit. Here, too, was a way to be
rid of slaves and export them out of the state at the
same time. Slave coffles moved regularly from Maryland and Virginia across the mountains into the West
and the Deep South. The slave had become too valuable to be set free.

The reinvigorated slave system not only gave slave owners a renewed faith in the future of the institution, drying up one motive for manumission, but also undermined the status of the free black. For if slavery was to continue to be a fact of life, or indeed a positive good, then the presence of a free-black population could serve only as a potential threat to order. On the one hand, free blacks, never conceived of as equal to whites or part of a community of equals, would always be an aggrieved class, potential revolutionaries. On the other hand, slaves would be disorderly only if they could imagine a possible status other than slavery. So during a period of the greatest national expansion and extension of liberty and democracy in American history, blacks, both slave and free, experienced a closing in and restriction. It would seem that white freedom and power depended on blacks being limited in both.

Free blacks exacerbated the fear of social unrest in two ways. As "free" persons in a nominally free society, their normal expectations would be for access to the condition of citizenship. They would presume to vote, demand a social voice, want to hold political office, own property, wield the power attached to wealth, and compete with whites. A truly free black man might well, in time, presume to exercise authority over white men, and that would undermine a fundamental social order in which class differences were subordinated to race. Second, one might imagine that free blacks would have natural sympathy with the plight of slaves. Most had been slaves; and while there might be some who would make much of their free condition, disdaining those who remained enslaved, most would see their own improvement tied to the bettering of the lot of the slave. Others, indeed, would grow bitter from the cramped

and limited nature of their own freedom and become
provocators of unrest.

By mid-century, there was a significant free-black
population in the South, mainly in the Upper South and
in the cities. But the Deep South, especially in cities
like Charleston and New Orleans, had sizable numbers
too. These individuals were anomalies. They had never
been granted full participation as citizens. In one place
or another, in the early years, free blacks were known
to have voted, but it was a rare and tenuous matter.
Free blacks were also known to own property, in some
cases considerable holdings, and some even owned
slaves as laborers. But all this was exceptional, a bit
strange. Freedom was a privilege, not a right; and free
blacks could not assume the legal certainty in their
property or in their security that whites took for
granted.

As the society became "democratic" in spirit and assumptions, the free black's status deteriorated. Uncertainty about the value of contract would make it difficult for him to do business. If injured, he would find it
nearly impossible to get court relief, since his testimony
was invalid against that of white men. Yet the witness
of slaves would be accepted against him. As white artisans claimed their racial right to be free of demeaning
competition with blacks, free-black craftsmen and
workers were restricted in the labor market. Some
would come to wonder if slavery were not a better condition than the kind of freedom they were permitted.

From the first definition of Africans as slave labor,
freeing and improving the condition of white servants,
those blacks who managed to slip through the net and
avoid being someone's property were anomalies. They

were not really free people in terms of the society; rather, they were black people who were not owned.

Most of the free blacks of the colonial period, and most of those in the Deep South, were the children, grandchildren, and great-grandchildren of slave owners. If not, their freedom had come because the slaveholder favored one or two of his slaves. As it was quite possible to maintain family relations, black and white, over several generations, some free black families remained under the protection of a white family. It also happened, more frequently than anyone can say, that the blending of blood continued, and persons of African descent disappeared into the white population with perhaps only furtive whispers echoing over the years.

Colonial settlement had begun in the seventeenth century with the same assumptions of social stratification that had existed in the Old World. There would be men of rank and privilege—wealthy and powerful persons who of right ought to govern—and there would be the lower orders—servants with neither property nor standing who of right ought to serve and obey. White men, of course, were in the higher rank, but whites also were in the lower. Few would have argued that it should have been otherwise. Such distinctions were done away with, at least in principle, when the enslavement of Africans made the fundamental social division racial rather than class. That was already a fact of colonial life. But the Revolution and subsequent national development intensified this trend.

The Revolution had not promised democracy, but by the beginning of the nineteenth century, the attack on privilege and rank and class among whites was well launched. Conservative features of society, such as property qualification for voting, were easy victims in Western states like Kentucky and Tennessee. Wherever the artifacts of class distinction eroded, there was a corresponding need to sharpen community definition so that blacks were clearly outside with no access to political power in the democracy. Where there had been propertied free blacks who exercised the vote in earlier days, by mid-century it was unthinkable in the South and much of the North that a black man could vote or hold office.

So the free black, like his brother in chains, was pushed beyond the pale, strengthening the illusion of equality and unity among whites. Of course, there were many whites of middling and poor circumstance. Ironically, the system of racial slavery depressed them even more than might have been the case in a class society, for in a white man's country that was free, democratic, and open, poverty was a disgrace rather than a circumstance.

Free blacks remained for whites a constant reminder of how easily one could lose his identity with his culture and civilization. Free mulattoes were living evidence of the compromise to racial integrity that would likely result from unguarded liberty. Already in numbers, much of the Southern population was as black as white. Without unrelenting white dominion, the society would cease being a white society at all. It would succumb to the laxity of those tropical peoples in its midst, losing its European character. There was so much outside that threatened civilization: the newness of the country, the rapid change of institutions and social order, the roughness of things that bred a kind of wildness. Blacks were just one of the elements. Stereotyped as the mirror opposite of all civilized traits—laziness, intemperance, passion, lust, childishness—they were defined as what the respectable Euro-American should not be. If Afro-Americans were essential to the society, it would be best to keep them confined as slaves. The free black weakened white men's confidence that the new world being built was, indeed, their own.

Such anxieties were another dimension of white concern for order. It was not just fear of uprisings and violence; it was also fear of the kind of natural accommodation toward which humans were inclined. Such anxieties made whites insist that whatever free-black population there was be managed and controlled as an alien group. That explains the growing concern that free blacks have no political voice, that their ability to hold property be circumscribed. Indeed, almost everywhere a black person was presumed a slave merely on evidence of color. Unless he had proof that he was free, or unless some white person would step forward to testify to his freedom, he stood to lose what little there was in being a free person of color. He would be advertised as a fugitive; and if no one claimed him, he would be sold as a slave.

A black person's freedom, especially in the slave states, was always precarious. Becoming the cause of a legal action, falling into debt, and being obliged to make long-term contracts for his labor were routes back into slavery. If a black person was without work, he would likely be taken up and auctioned off under vagrancy statutes. And it was an ever-present danger that he be kidnapped and transported into slavery in another place. His best protection from all of these dangers was to have a white patron.

Being neither slave nor free, the free black found himself economically between two stools. The work of a slave society was done by slaves. Free blacks, therefore, had to compete with slave labor for the work that existed. In dangerous work, the free black was gen-

erally preferred to slaves, whose loss would be costly
to an owner. Otherwise, slave labor was preferred.
Sometimes it was thought desirable to hire free labor
because it need not be supported when work ended. In
any case, slavery depreciated labor such that one could
charge very little for it.

On the other hand, where a white laboring class
emerged, there was generally a successful denial to
blacks of those occupations whites would hold. Native
and immigrant white labor were able to push blacks out
of skilled occupations they had formerly held. In the
cities of the Upper South, there was a constant erosion
of the place of free blacks in skilled crafts and trades;
nor could they venture into areas that whites occu-
pied. All whites would seem to have agreed that it was
unseemly for whites to be held to competition with
blacks. Consequently, those occupations that were
menial or suggested a body-servant were accepted as
work for black people. Whites who would hire blacks to
do work considered suitable for white men were challenged lest they deprive white men and their families
of a livelihood. Free blacks could manage only as they
were able to underbid white labor, pressing themselves
thus further into a marginal existence.

Free blacks were also shoved into the corners of
Southern social life. While from the earliest colonial
times they attended white churches, they were often
segregated into "Negro" pews or into the balconies. The
evangelical denominations—Methodist and Baptist—
at first made little or no distinction between white and
black worshipers, even supporting black preachers in
mixed or white churches. But by the early nineteenth
century, the trend toward separation affected them as
well, and the underlying brotherhood in Christ suc-

cumbed to popular pressure that whites and blacks would be better brothers in the next world than in this one.

Free blacks moved toward the establishment of their own churches, persuaded by the different temperament and style of black religion and by the desire to be rid of the constant affronts they experienced in white churches. Black Methodists and Baptists, in particular, moved into formally separate denominations such as the African Methodist Episcopal Church or, short of that, held separate meetings from the white congregation. All this was done against considerable white pressure, for although whites did not want to join with blacks in an integrated fellowship, they were even more uneasy with the evidence of black separate organization and independence. Such anxiety and hostility led to the outlawing of the African Church in Charleston after the Denmark Vesey conspiracy.

Free blacks organized for self-help in other ways. Always placing a high value on education, they were, nonetheless, excluded from white schools. Through all the Southern cities there were efforts, often sporadic and futile, to establish African schools. However, burdened by long hours of labor and low pay, few blacks could afford the time or the money for education. In addition, the schools suffered greatly from white pressure against them. They were often closed and founders run out of town, but the educational effort was kept alive by individual courage.

Free blacks also organized societies for self-improvement. There were lodges that provided opportunity for study and conviviality among their members. There were burial societies, which collectively relieved the costs of funerals and, at the same time, provided something of the pomp and ceremony that gave the funeral

a deserved weight and importance. Often these societies, as was the case with the Brown Society of
Charleston, made class distinctions among free blacks
which, based on color, allowed the admission only of
mulattoes.

Between meaningful conditions—being neither slave
nor free—the free black felt the onus of race, its im-
puted slowness and backwardness being a reflection
upon him. To be accepted as a free man and advance
in the society, he would feel the need to show himself
exceptional, not like slaves or the poorer class of free
blacks. He would want to appear industrious, conservative, and safe. Whatever he thought about slavery, he
would be careful of what he said. To be accepted himself meant for him to accept reality. To identify with
white authority, to show himself in tune with "community" interests rather than those of his race, might
do more for the uplift of his people than to be run out
of the state as an abolitionist hothead. Free blacks'
strategies for survival were fraught with ambiguities and
contradictions. Where the community's sole criterion
was race, there was no way out but to be born again.

It was natural enough for some free blacks to see
their well-being as ultimately tied to white people.
There were, after all, informal ties of family: they were
blood kin often enough or they had been part of the
white "family." To nurture and maintain those associations, especially if the white family was influential, was
to have a white protector. That meant economic support, for even white laborers would retreat before a
powerful white family's defense of a black craftsman.

Identity with whites also manifested itself in efforts to
make class distinctions among free blacks. To be able,
because of favored position and income, to distinguish
between oneself and other blacks—poorer, without the

demeanor of modest propriety—would seem to give
status. Also, mulattoes could sometimes exploit favorable family connections. If it was privileged to be
white and base to be black, then to be one of the many
shades between brown and white meant having certain
pretensions. The mulattoes who came to the United
States as refugees from the Saint-Dominique uprisings
never tired of trying to establish the three-caste system
that characterized most of Latin America and the
Caribbean. However, the system failed to take hold in
the United States because white people were more comfortable with sharp racial distinctions. The failure of
this caste arrangement strengthened a sense among
Afro-Americans that they were one people.

Free blacks who were close to whites also took on
white social attitudes. Patrons of blacks were generally
wealthy and patrician, a class that could scarcely dis-
guise its contempt for middling and poor whites. Blacks
often shared those views as they sometimes possessed
the style and well-being that made them superior to
poor whites. They were better off, they were cultured,
they had a more decent lifestyle. Also poor whites,
desperately competing with slaves and free blacks for
their livelihood, were often the bitterest antagonists of
black folks. Being otherwise lowest in social esteem,
blacks enjoyed indulging in superior feelings around
patrician white folks. It was natural enough, but it foreshadowed a chronic enmity between blacks and the
only class of whites with whom they might have found
common interests.

In basic ways, however, the black attachment to
white folks rested on illusion. White folks, especially as
relatives of colored folks, were deeply ambivalent.
However much they were wiling to indulge and patron-
ize blacks, they were not prepared to accord them

status as free men. While a few would give lip service
to the notion that their black friends were as good as
most whites who were free, they were not prepared to
face down the weight of opinion that insisted on racial
division in the society. Thus, the few blacks who enjoyed the patronage of whites reaped benefits only as
far as that personal aegis extended and no further.
Even those like William Johnson of Natchez, a free
black man of considerable wealth who was the creditor
and friend of whites, had to walk a thin line, for the
power that he gained in money was as much a threat to
him as it was a means of security.

8

Adaptation Resistance, and Virtue

THE MAKING of the Afro-American people was a process blending the old with the new, changing the old into something that was new and that could survive a world in the making. For blacks, it was a world of narrowing limits, closed and oppressive. The adaptation took time. It was not that laws were laid down in the seventeenth century defining the Afro-Americans' condition forever. Those laws and early decisions by the Anglo-American rulers that blacks would be slaves merely set the broad terms under which the Afro-American world was to be shaped. What was to come in the next two centuries— the continued importation of Africans until 1808, and the growth and expansion of the slave economy—was as much the result of the active energy and intelligence of Afro-Americans as it was the pressure placed upon them by the system. They were not victims but an oppressed folk who found a way to create themselves as a people and a culture despite the odds against their doing so.

Theirs was more than mere survival of the biological

organism, involving a kind of tenacity and oafishness. The challenge was to maintain their humanity and their dignity under circumstances which would deny those qualities. Theirs was not a surrender to conditions but an effort to create room for the human spirit to live, this within an environment that would everywhere reduce that spirit to one of an animal. Many generations had to struggle to keep the faith.

On the eve of the Civil War, the realities of slave life were quite different from what they had been a century or more earlier. The differences were both in the people the Afro-Americans had become and in the terms of slave life. Much in the same way that the American nation and the Southern economy had been in the grip of change during the centuries between the colonial establishments and the expanding imperial nation, slaves had changed from an exotic people presumed to be external to society to Americans whose very presence defined that society.

The African who got off the boat in eighteenth-century America had the special problems of an immigrant and a slave. A person from a traditional and static order, he was to become part of a modern society whose underlying principle was change. A collective person wrenched from an intimate social context that gave a sense of self, he was thrust into one, against his will, which would isolate and atomize individuals one from another, undermining as far as could be done those collective institutions—family and religion—that might serve as a substitute context. Such an African immigrant's options were few: to find something within the new context that would give him meaning or to choose one of the many ways to die; to challenge the overwhelming power or to retreat into deep despondency.

In the early years, it was impossible to talk of an

Afro-American people or a slave community. There
was such a wide variety of peoples and experiences as
to limit the possibilities of cohesiveness. The Africans
in America had come from different peoples; and while
time blurred distinctions among them, they still sensed
deep within that Fulani was not Ibo or Fanti. Mixed
in with those whom the slave trade had brought directly
from Africa were the many who had first been slaves
in the West Indies, African as well as Island born. For
a time, American Indians and their progeny mixed with
white and black. And, at last, there were native-born
blacks, who grew in time to dominate slave life. Yet for
a full generation following the closing of the slave trade
in 1808, this heterogeneity remained a factor.

Blacks could in no sense feel "at home" with one
another as long as they were conscious of fundamental
cultural differences among themselves. However, by
the 1840s, except perhaps for those slaves drawn into
French Creole and Catholic cultures in Louisiana and
those isolated on the sea islands of South Carolina and
Georgia, the slave could be said to be of one people and
one culture. A slave who made the trek in a slave coffle
from the Upper South to Alabama, Mississippi, Texas,
or Arkansas while suffering the pain of separation from
family and friends in the old place, could find in the
new place people much like himself. Some might even
have come from his home. He would find plantation
life much like the place he left.

This evolvement of an Afro-American people occurred within a changing America: political independence, rapid expansion and migration to the West,
intermittent Indian wars, and the incorporation of all
lands east of the Great Plains. The basic, aggressive
tendencies of the American people were well established
by mid-century. A labor system that once might have

been thoughtlessly accepted or, later, tentatively tolerated was by the 1840s part of the nation's grain.

Southern life had become relatively stable during the
two decades preceding the Civil War. The rapidly expanding frontier was settling into an ordered society
that would give slaves their best chance of finding
greater security for their families and of extending their
living space by seeking modifications of conventional
treatment. To the extent that they were able to gain
space and some protection of the self from willfulness
and capriciousness, they had something to guard and
protect. Paradoxically, their adaptations and minor
victories became the basis for a conservatism that would
not risk everything for symbolic acts of defiance.

The first test of adaptation for the newly arrived African had been to overcome those pressures that pulled
him within himself. He would have to open himself to
the possibility of learning. There were new tongues to
be sorted out, organized, and reduced to common signs.
There was the need to allow oneself to remember skills
—the working of the soil or wood, the weaving of
baskets and cloth, the tending of animals—and to be
willing to give one's mind and talent to an alien and
threatening enterprise. There was the need to learn new
skills and new ways—often rudely forced—in order to
be allowed to live a meaningful life. Africans would be
dragged brutally into labor, and they would relent willingly or reluctantly, but they would do it or die.

So the African's choices were narrow. He could retreat into himself, giving only the minimum part of himself to the life around him and, by the same token,
taking in only what was forced upon him. Withdrawn
and dispirited, he would lend himself neither to the life
around him nor to those defiant slaves who would challenge their common condition. Or, he could try to

escape into the wilderness, to the Indians perhaps, or
to nowhere in particular, just to be gone. Or, he could
strike out with his hands or any other slight weapon that
his hands could find. Others would watch as he was
hanged, burned at the stake, maimed, dismembered,
decapitated, or as he suffered the contrivances of torture. His head on a roadside stake might be a lasting
reminder to others of his folly. Resistance, coming from
the will to defy and say an everlasting no to oppression,
ended most often in death. There were more than a few
whose pride would demand they pay that awesome
price. Yet something in the human spirit voted for life
rather than death, even though there would be a price
to be paid for living. After all proper due is given to
the defiant ones, it is to the vast majority who adapted,
doing what they could to sustain their humanity despite
the cost, that the Afro-American people owe their history.

The changing historical circumstances of the slave
system determined the limits of adaptation. Mobility
and expansion in the South meant that Southern plantation life remained marginal and uncertain into the
nineteenth century. The early confusion of white, black,
and Indian in the servant class, before servitude and
slavery were made synonymous with blackness, confounded identity. Oppressed together, red, white, and
black found common cause from time to time in the
early years, and it would take a while for blacks to
know slavery as their exclusive lot.

The historian Gerald Mullin tells us that successful
breaks from slavery in the eighteenth century were dependent upon an individualism that had to be acquired
over time. Such a break required a highly adapted slave
who knew the English language well, who commanded
some skill that would be currency abroad, who was

familiar with the country—the cities, roads, and water-ways—that he could make his way, not as a stranger but as one who had a goal and knew how to reach it. He would have to be able to talk his way out of difficulties, if caught; he would need a lot of answers ready on his tongue. Such a slave had a fair chance of escaping and blending into the society as a free black. But such talents presupposed a willingness to make oneself a part of a new culture.

Most slaves did not have these qualities of individual-ism, nor in the early years was it possible for them to sustain an African community identity. Where there happened to be a coincidence of tribal connections, several might escape together, often with no destination in mind, sometimes hoping to find a way back to Africa. Others fled with whites. But most blacks who broke away in the eighteenth century would merely lie out in the neighborhood wilderness or try to join with Indians. To slip away and find a new home was possible, for the woods and swamps and caves were hiding places and living places too.

There were those who would find the harness bind-ing, cutting into the flesh; but as the body survived and as there was pleasure in society, they would accommo-date themselves. Others, however, could not be held to confinements of any kind. They found isolation in caves or swamps preferable to the society of slaves. These maroons (as they were called) gathered as a group in a hideaway. Sometimes they planted crops for them-selves, but for the most part they raided plantations, got food from slaves, or stole it from the storehouses. All the while, they had to be on guard lest they be found by the patrols that regularly searched for them. The officials called them outlaws, and they would likely be killed on sight. Nevertheless, despite the danger, isolation, and the wildness imposed by fugitive life, maroon colonies persisted through much of Southern history. One maroon, Bras Coupé of Louisiana, became so formidable as to leave his mark in legend and folklore, frightening the imaginations of white and black, children and adults.

In the early years, when Indian villages were just beyond the country settled by planters, plantation life involved a mix in which Indians were drawn into the system as slaves. They intermarried with black and white, and were, in time, to blend into the Afro-American population. Free Indians interacted with blacks in other ways, as both antagonists and allies. Many slaves who broke away from plantation life found refuge among Indian peoples, becoming part of their tribes, intermarrying, and losing themselves among native Americans. But blacks could not always trust Indians. Just as some blacks joined with whites in wars against Indians, some Indians could always be counted on to capture fugitive slaves and return them for a price. Yet, the Indian presence enlarged the possibilities of African adaptation in the New World. Once the Indian was removed from the East, an important option was withdrawn from the slave.

At least until the second decade of the nineteenth century, there was a non-Anglo-American presence along the southern border of Georgia. It took some doing but refugees from Georgia and the Carolinas could make their way into foreign territory. From time to time, depending upon the Spanish colony's relationship with the Anglo-Americans, slaves could find refuge in Florida. This rendered Florida a place of great uncertainty to slaveholders in the Lower South. After 1819, however, when Florida was ceded to the United States, another route of escape was cut off, and the realities of Afro-American life became just that much more restricted.

The Stono uprising in South Carolina dramatized the style of resistance possible when the country was young enough to offer options outside settled regions and the slave population was varied enough to create disorder. Stono was singular in scale, in the numbers of slaves involved. It was one of a pattern of less dramatic episodes where smaller groups tried, and sometimes succeeded, in getting out of the country.

Through much of 1739, South Carolinians were very troubled by the numbers of slaves who managed to desert the colony, finding their way to the Spanish fort at St. Augustine. Such defections had always been a problem, but it seemed that the numbers were increasing and the refugees becoming bolder. The Spanish king had issued an edict in 1733 granting freedom to black fugitives from the British colonies, but it was five years before the Spaniards in Florida acted. Then they began to offer asylum to fugitives from the British colony rather than return them as the Anglo-Americans wanted, or sell them, as had been their habit. The king's edict, published in St. Augustine in 1738, was broadcast by drum to all the St. Augustine blacks, and eventually reached slaves in South Carolina through ship crews arriving in Charleston harbor. Thus, there was reason enough for the upswing in slave defections from South Carolina and reason for white anxiety as well.

On Sunday, September 9, 1739, about twenty slaves gathered twenty miles from Charleston, on the Stono River, raided a store for guns and ammunition, and began their trek southward toward Georgia and St. Augustine. Along the way they burned houses, killing whites within and securing more weapons and supplies. As they marched, their ranks swelled with black recruits until there were well over fifty.

After a march of more than ten miles, they paused in a field, grouping themselves, dancing, and beating drums in an effort to attract more slaves. They were confident they could make it to St. Augustine, and their numbers led them to believe that they could overcome any opposition they might encounter.

However, they were caught off guard by armed and mounted whites. Those blacks who were not killed in the first skirmish or who managed to escape were summarily killed and their heads set upon mileposts along the road. The hunt for the remaining escapees continued for weeks, and it was a month before whites would declare the uprising at its end.

What Stono illustrates is the special circumstances adhering to slavery in early American history. Here was an uprising by slaves with a realistic objective: refuge in a foreign province. Furthermore, it demonstrated that African tribal identification was still possible among them, for the conspirators were largely Angolan. They had probably gained word of the Spanish edict through black seamen, by drums, and by word of mouth. At a crucial point in their escape, they danced and drummed messages to other blacks. Such behavior could not have been imagined in the nineteenth century.

Peter H. Wood's history of slavery in colonial South Carolina points to another distinguishing feature of this event. Blacks were a majority of South Carolina's population at the time of Stono. The ability of whites to control the colony of black slaves had become dubious, and Stono was a shocking signal of alarm to the master class. Thus, Wood marks Stono as a turning point in that colony's history. Subsequently, great attention would be given to shifting the proportion of whites to blacks so that white control could be insured.

Stono was a turning point in another way. South Carolinians were successful in getting Governor James Edward Oglethorpe and the Georgians to police more rigorously the most convenient passages through that colony to Florida. After Stono, what had been an available escape route became hazardous. South Carolina blacks knew they would have to fight their way to freedom across miles of territory patroled by hostile whites and Indians, eager for a bounty on fugitives' scalps and ears. Following Stono the pattern would change, for the fugitives would have to plot how to arm themselves for a lengthy struggle toward freedom. The immediate targets of rebels would become the town of Charleston and its storehouses. Such plans were far more complicated and problematic than flight across the country to Florida. In time, all frontiers would be closed or too distant for escape. What tactics would serve then?

As long as there remained an option to escape Anglo-American society, there were always many who would take the chance. As in the flights to St. Augustine, it was not just the escape of individuals to freedom but an escape to some presumed social order. Whereas some would always prefer life in the wilderness as a maroon to that of a slave, most who would escape chose a destination that offered an established social context. This was crucial. He who would be a fugitive might have ample cause to flee the place where he was held enslaved, but a thoughtful person would have to know that he was running to some place. Otherwise, out there, beyond the plantation and the hostile white society, there might seem a void, an emptiness where one might survive, but alone.

A century after the Stono uprising, a variation of this

problem presented itself in the black and Indian alliance in the Seminole War of 1835. This guerrilla war, which raged intermittently for almost ten years, was ostensibly over the Seminoles' refusal to follow their parent tribe, the Creeks, to lands west of the Mississippi that had been allotted to them by the federal government. Much of the pressure for removal came from the expansion of Southern agriculture and the unwillingness of planters to have Indians in the vicinity. Naturally, there were racist reasons: it was to be a white man's country. Yet, more practically, Indian tribes and villages always stood as an attractive alternative to their slaves. As long as Indians were about, slave owners would have to worry about negotiating for the return of escaped slaves.

In fact, some of the principal Seminole leaders and interpreters who fought and sustained the war were Afro-Americans. Many had come into the tribes in the days of Spanish Florida, many belonged to the tribes as slaves, but a great number were refugees from Anglo-American slaveholders in Georgia and Florida. A major cause for the continued hostilities was the refusal of the Seminoles to turn blacks over to those whites who would claim them as slaves. Southern whites and slave traders were torn between their strong desire to have the Indians removed from Florida without delay and their insistence on making claims against blacks among the Seminoles.

When the war waxed in favor of the Indians, it was not uncommon for them to raid plantations and take away slaves who wanted to leave. Although Indian territory seemed an attractive redoubt to many slaves in southern Florida and Georgia, the hardships of life and warfare in the swamps caused many escaped and captured slaves to return to their enslavement of their own will. The Indian presence was a nuisance to white men everywhere in the United States, but it was a potentially subversive element where slavery persisted. As long as there was a way out that provided a social viability, most slaves would snatch at it even if the risks were enormous.

By the 1840s and 1850s, a little more than a generation after the importation of slaves from abroad had been made illegal, slave life had changed considerably from what it had been in the eighteenth century. No longer were slaves an alien, displaced, or wandering people. The slaves and the land, their lives and labor, had come to belong to one another, like all serfs and peasants, ironically more a part of the country than those who owned them both. They were the land's, while the land belonged to their masters.

Ethnic distinctions had been lost. At least the wide varieties of African peoples and tongues, known in the eighteenth century, were gone. Even West Indians were no longer an unintegrated part of the population. And the events and traumas of Saint-Dominique were as remote in memory as the American Revolution. The basic distinction had been made: black people and slaves were one thing, white people were something else. So, while degrees of skill and learning varied among slaves, and while those blacks with white blood might sometimes have pretensions, they were one people: Afro-Americans, Negroes, people of color. When one looked into the faces of others, always there would be the recognition of a common experience and a common destiny.

The great flux and change that had poured people in slave coffles and trains across the mountains and into the Deep South had slowed. Settlements and families had been sundered in the declining Upper South, and the migration of black people helped to develop the new regions that were labor hungry. They would not have chosen to move; they were forced to. The profit that was calculated in the new land was for others. For slaves there was loss—of parents, spouse, or children. But by the 1850s, the pulse of that change was less rapid, less compulsive. While anxiety about disruption, sale, and removal remained with all slaves, most could now hope to remain in one place. Insecurity, nevertheless, was chronic, because one's destiny was in the hands of others. The insecurity itself—the not knowing for certain how long before some friend would be taken away—made slaves care more for one another than was typical of most people in American society. They came to cherish their world for as long as they could hold it together.

Relative stability meant that institutions could take hold among them. Slaves transformed Christianity to serve their needs. Black religion could never have been articulated with such fullness and character without a reasonable order among slaves. It was the white master's religion, true enough, and some among them would continue to ridicule the white Jesus and the white God. But others converted that religion to serve themselves, and it at least provided a common ethos that could tie them together in a way that the various African religions of their forebears could not.

Relative stability encouraged expectations of the system and the setting of standards of behavior, which the master and his overseers might have done well to honor. Slave owners were forever publishing their acquired wisdom on the care and treatment of slaves. As the system matured, they tended to stress ordered routine, clear and reasonable expectations, respect for the slaves' sensibilities, and admonishment for humane treatment. While these were always written in language suggesting masters to be the sole authors of such intelligence, it was the historical push and shove of experience between master and slave that produced this wisdom. The slaves played an enormous part in the modification of conditions. The conventional wisdom of slave management resulted more from the pressure of slaves than from the detached judgment of masters.

Although oppressed, the slaves created for themselves room to live as a people. They squeezed out tenuous respect for family. They tried to define a "normal" work load in terms of what had always been done. They laid claim to time off on Sundays and traditional holidays around Christmas. In silent and subtle ways they allowed the master to know that they had expectations of him, that their duty implied a duty on his part. While they could not strike or rebel effectively, they could and did make their grievances known; and their masters often lived to regret failing their trust.

All this is to say that adaptation and adjustment came from within a mutually understood system. By the mid-nineteenth century these slaves were native Americans, trying to make their homes better, even under cramped circumstances. Gone were the options to do otherwise. Except in the backwoods of Arkansas or near the Texas border with Mexico, where slaves crossed a national border, there was no longer a possibly hospitable society into which to flee. Yet opportunity for escape remained for slaves of the Upper South, and growing numbers took advantage of it. Most of them had to go as far as Canada to be wholly free of the tyranny of the slave system. Except for these, the great hope for Afro-American slaves was in what collectively they could make of an oppressive condition.

It is within this context of growing stability and order that we must view the slave resistance of the nineteenth century. The opportunities for effective resistance diminished as time went on, and the expanded sense of room and livable conditions, however meager, intensified the sense of risk. Slaves could believe they had something to protect and something to lose.

The nineteenth century opened with perhaps the most daring and forthright slave attempt to overthrow the system. In the late summer of 1800, Gabriel Prosser, a slave, led a broad-based conspiracy to take Richmond, Virginia. The insurrection would have involved the largest slave army in the history of the country, and it appears to have been the most carefully planned and thoughtful slave revolt. Estimates run to several thousand slaves who had been enlisted in the effort, and Prosser had carefully marked out the targets in Richmond first to be taken.

Armed with swords, scythes, guns, and pikes, the black army was to march on Richmond in three columns, one capturing the arsenal, another taking the powder house to secure weapons and deprive the enemy of them, and the third forming a pincers on the city, attacking it from both ends with orders to kill all white people except Methodists, Frenchmen, and Quakers. With Richmond in their hands, they were to attack other Virginia cities, gaining slave support on the way.

The ultimate goal of Prosser and his followers was the conversion of Virginia territory, perhaps the entire state itself, from a slave society into a free one. Failing this, it would appear that Prosser would have led his army into the mountains to sustain a guerrilla war.

It was a daring plan. But, given its scale, it was impossible to maintain secrecy among over a thousand persons who were spread across the countryside. Even though whites were apprehensive that something was in the air, the secret was kept for several months until the very day of the planned attack, when two slaves informed their masters of the plot.

Even so, if several thousand slaves had attacked Richmond on August 30, according to plan, their chances against a hastily gathered defense would have been good. They would have lost an element of surprise, costing them casualties perhaps, but whites would have been hard pressed to overcome such a large army with clear targets.

What defeated Prosser's army was not the breach of secrecy but a fortuitous cloudburst and thunderstorms. which wracked the Richmond area on that fateful Saturday. About a thousand men did make the appointed rendezvous, only to be forced to turn back at the Brook Swamp bridge, which had become impassable. It was a delay that was fateful to the rebellion, for now the intelligence given by the slave informers could be put to use. White authorities immediately rounded up the known leaders. Within a week thirty-five rebels, including Gabriel Prosser, were executed. Efforts to gain further information from the captives were fruitless; thus no others were implicated. By the end of October, this extraordinary slave rebellion had been thwarted.

Twenty-two years later, a black conspiracy to take the city of Charleston, South Carolina, was also foiled, certainly the consequence of betrayal by some black men. The story is confusing because the putative leader of the plot, Denmark Vesey, and his lieutenants went to their executions revealing neither their purpose, plans, nor confederates. It is hard to credit all the testimony in the record of the trial that followed the hanging of these leaders, for much of its was obviously self-serving. Many blacks, seeing the game was up and detecting the clear eagerness of whites to uncover a broad conspiracy, might well have imagined that their lives depended on telling even more than might have been true. Their white inquisitors were not particular about actual truth as long as the confessions satisfied their suspicions. Calculated or not, those who told the most fanciful stories were more apt to escape with their lives than those who pleaded innocence, whatever the truth.

Apparently, a conspiracy had been brewing for several months. There were supposed to have been thousands of blacks involved at one level or another. Arms and powder had been stolen and cached away, poles and spikes manufactured. Yet no one seemed to know the specifics of the plot. Probably, Vesey and his closest lieutenant kept those details to themselves, expecting to reveal final plans as the chosen date approached—variously given as July 4 and the second Sunday of that month. Great care was taken to minimize the effect of any betrayal. The army seemed organized in cells so that no one knew the names of all involved. Denmark Vesey, Peter Poyas, Mingo Harth, and Gullah Jack were the central conspirators, but beyond them there were only vague assumptions as to numbers.

The leaders had wanted to keep recruitment in their own hands for fear of betrayal. Failure to do that proved to be fatal. William Paul, a slave unauthorized to recruit, was overheard trying to enlist another on Charleston's wharf. Paul was arrested and held in the "hole of the prison" until he, fearful that he was to be hanged, told the story of a grand slave conspiracy aimed at the killing of all whites. So fantastic was his story yet so empty of specific names and details, that the authorities dismissed it as fearful hysteria.

On the fourteenth of June, two weeks after Paul's arrest, a white man reported a rumored plot centering in the African Church. According to his information, an uprising was to occur on the sixteenth. After that date had passed without incident, ten blacks were arrested, including Denmark Vesey and Peter Poyas, class leaders at the church. Vesey and Poyas were silent throughout their trial, but they were convicted on the confession of one of the prisoners. They were hanged on July 2.

It was only after the trial and execution of the group arrested with Vesey that the grand trial for conspiracy took place as a sort of inquest into the full dimensions of the plot. But the inquiry was carried on in a witch-hunt-like atmosphere, where clever blacks knew that the safest path was to continue to excite the imagination of the inquisitors, telling them everything—more than everything. It is impossible to know the truth. In all, thirty-five slaves were put to death, thirty-two were ordered transported or sold away beyond the United States, eleven were recommended to be transported by their masters, fifteen were acquitted, and thirty-eight were discharged without prejudice. Those who were most forthcoming with acceptable testimony did manage to avoid execution, although they were sentenced to be transported. John Paul, the owner of William, was urged to transport the slave whose initial carelessness and hysterical confession had set the stage for the debacle.

It is difficult to know what Denmark Vesey's plans were. Apparently, he wanted to take Charleston, attacking in the summer when most whites would have moved out of the city. He would have killed all those who were caught. From there it is hard to guess. He was aware of the Haitian Republic. He had been a seaman before winning his freedom in a lottery. He spoke French and Spanish, and his contact with seamen in the Charleston port had kept him in touch with the world outside. It was said that Vesey had tried to communicate with Haiti, hoping to retreat there after the successful uprising. It was also said that he hoped to get aid from the British, a fanciful notion if so, even though it had only been seven years since the end of hostilities between the United States and Britain.

Nat Turner's revolt differed from Gabriel Prosser's and Denmark Vesey's in two important respects: it was not directed at a city as the principal target, and it was neither massive in number nor intricately planned. Ironically, as Marion D. Kilson has pointed out, its very smallness in scale and impulsiveness in character allowed Turner's plan to advance beyond the stage of conspiracy to become action, making it the most devastating of all.

Nat Turner was an inspired man. He had lived in Southampton, Virginia, all of his thirty-one years, was a skilled craftsman and a devout preacher with an evangelical genius. He was also a brooding and thoughtful man, open to the passion of the Christian religion. He had long sensed himself to have a special calling and was given to seeing visions.

The first and most dramatic of these occurred in 1825, when he saw black and white spirits battling in the heavens and heard voices charging him with his call. He was to take up the burden as prophet. He had seen into God's plan, and he was to hold himself ready to be God's instrument.

Turner pulled himself more into his privateness, continually contemplating his charge: what did it mean? On May 12, 1828, he heard another heavenly voice telling him that "the Serpent was loosened, and Christ had laid down the yoke he had borne for the sins of men." Turner was being called to take up the fight against the serpent, "for the time is fast approaching when the first should be last and last should be first." He was told to keep his secret until another sign.

A solar eclipse occurred in February 1831. The seal was removed from his lips, and he took four trusted slaves into his confidence. They planned to begin their attack on July 4. But as the day approached, the plans and strategies were discussed and changed several times until Turned fell ill and was unable to act on the appointed day. On the thirteenth of August, the sun appeared bluish green throughout the day. Turner, taking this as another sign, planned to meet with his comrades on the twenty-first. Apparently, word went beyond the small group, because on the day they were to begin they were joined by another man, not recruited by Turner, who wanted to take part. The six men planned through the night and attacked their first home at two o'clock, the morning of the twenty-second.

It was the house of Turner's master, William Travis. They killed the entire family, for the plan was to kill whites without regard to age or sex until the men were sufficiently terrorized. Then their women and children could be spared along with those who offered no resistance. Following the attack on the Travis household, Turner put his small band through military drills in the Travis yard. Then they proceeded through the county.

They went from house to house, killing white inhabitants as they came upon them, using broad ax, sword, or shot. They by-passed one house whose poor white inhabitants "thought no better of themselves than the Negroes." It is said that they may have intentionally by-passed others. On their way, they gathered recruits from the slaves, and they took horses and weapons.

Their numbers grew through the night until they totaled about seventy men, mostly mounted.

It was about noon on the twenty-second that Nat Turner decided to attack the town of Jerusalem, which was about three miles from their advanced position. There, Turner hoped to get weapons and powder. The alarm, however, had long since been sounded through the county; and while Turner and part of his party paused at the place of James Parker, they were attacked by white men riding from Jerusalem. The whites were at first repulsed, but reinforced, they finally managed to scatter Turner's army.

Nat Turner and about forty men hid overnight in the country, but a false alarm reduced his force to twenty by the twenty-third. With this small force, he attacked the place of a Dr. Blunt, where the slaves were said to be part of the resistance. Turner's force was repulsed. By that evening, Turner was alone. He hid in the woods, in a cave he had dug. He managed to survive for two months, thus.

By the time Nat Turner was captured and placed in the Jerusalem jail, many who were purported to have been with him had been tried and sentenced. The figures are unclear, but aside from those who might have been killed in combat, it appears that sixteen had been hanged following a trial, seven convicted and transported, seventeen discharged or acquitted, and four free blacks held for further trial. Turner himself came to trial, was convicted and hanged, leaving what purports to be a confession, full and detailed, a unique document in the history of slavery in the United States.

It is difficult to know what Nat Turner's plans were. He was too secretive, giving his closest lieutenants little sense of his ultimate objective, other, that is to say, than that they were striking for liberty. We can suspect from

the character of his visions that he saw slavery not only
as a personal and racial affront but as a sin against God.
The issue for him was not personal liberty. He had, in
1821, successfully escaped, returning voluntarily after
thirty days. With his fluency and quickness of mind, he
probably could have made a successful escape. He
claimed that he returned because voices had warned
him against thinking only of things of this world. He
had a higher calling than personal freedom. After his
return in 1821, it was only a matter of time before he
would take up the yoke that Christ had cast down.

The visions, as described in the "Confessions," are
clear in calling for a revolutionary act, not mere resistance or escape but an attack on local authority and the
slaughter of white people. The word was that "the last
should be first and the first last." The slaves involved
were fighting for their liberty, it is true; slavery was the
target, but Nat Turner's object was cosmic.

It seemed unnecessary for him to have a clear strategy once the first blow was struck and the action was set
in motion. The act itself was divinely inspired, and
doubtless he knew that the will of God would act
through him as a prophet. That is not to say that his
attack was thoughtless. He was very careful to hold
himself aloof as the leader through what otherwise
might have been utter chaos. He wanted to drill his
men. He seemed conscious of the use of terror as an
element of attack. As soon as his ranks were swelled
enough he was ready for an attack on the town of Jerusalem. But beyond that, there was no target or strategy
that can be made out. The object was in the action itself: it was a millennial vision.

Attempting to impose a goal and a practical strategy
on Nat Turner, some have assumed that he would have
proceeded to the great Dismal Swamp, from which spot

he could carry on guerrilla attacks. But there is nothing to support that scheme. Turner himself evaded capture for two months, but he never left the area where the revolt had taken place. He hid in caves that he had dug, went out at night to overhear what was happening and to get food. He made no effort in all that time to put distance between himself and his hunters, perhaps gaining his freedom in the end. It would seem that until his capture he was waiting for the right moment to take up the sword once again and complete what had been frustrated. After all, he had had no word that his prophetic mission had been withdrawn.

Throughout his months of hiding, the entire region was being terrorized by military units, vigilante groups, and nondescript whites whose hysteria had driven them to stamp out every suspicion of rebellion. Blacks everywhere were being beaten, shot, hanged, and terrorized. No one was safe. But this would not have surprised Nat Turner: surely the army of the "serpent" was a vicious foe and would not die easy. Perhaps it was just this kind of indiscriminate terror against blacks that would convert them to hate as well as fear and make them ready to move when the prophet reappeared.

Although there is no evidence for it, it is hard to believe that Turner hid in the neighborhood for two months without making contact with other slaves for food or information. If so, it was never disclosed, and it suggests the possibility that there may have been some few who would protect him, support him, and perhaps even follow him in due time.

Apparently, Turner never doubted his visions. He never thought that he had been deceived or that he had deceived himself. According to the "Confessions," when he was asked about his calling in the light of his failure, capture, and impending execution, he replied. "Was not Christ crucified?"

Nat Turner's vision was correct, although he did not see the end of it. There was a scourge in the land with white against black and much blood flowing. While it began with Turner and his army killing between fifty-five and sixty-five whites, its aftermath resulted in the deaths of hundreds of blacks. The white hysteria extended across the South, with reports of suspected uprisings and conspiracies in places as remote as Kentucky. Laws were passed throughout the South further restricting the liberty of both free blacks and slaves, and repressive old laws were resurrected with a new resolve to enforce them. Southern blacks at the time might have had reason to curse Nat Turner and his rebellion; but in another decade, his name would represent defiance and sacrifice, a hatred of slavery. He would remain a viable symbol through the next century, belying the accusation that slaves were submissive or cowardly. Some have said, with reason, that Turner's vision ended in the debacle of the Civil War thirty years after he was hanged, and some would see it as a sword still poised over the American nation.

Gabriel Prosser, Denmark Vesey, and Nat Turner were remarkably different in style and character from the resisters of an earlier time. They were not arsonists or maroons, nor were they "freedom fighters" escaping tyranny into a foreign land, political refugees like the men at Stono. They were Americans, and they saw that their fate was to be worked out on the ground on which they stood.

Gabriel Prosser had clearly been inspired by the ideology of the American Revolution, which had ended only seventeen years before his attempted coup. Certainly his rhetoric was filled with references to the "rights of man" and apostrophes about liberty or death. His plan was to take Richmond and much of Virginia, and to create there a new republic. To Gabriel Prosser and his insurrectionists, they were merely taking their land and claiming their birthright. Denmark Vesey, too, meant to take and hold Charleston as a means of claiming his place and his liberty. Not being a native-born American and having been a seaman in his youth, Vesey's own vision extended beyond the continent; he found inspiration in Haiti. But it is also said that he was provoked by the national debate over Missouri, where the South made its first major defense of slavery, posing itself against "free societies." Vesey's central role in the establishment of the African Methodist Church attests to his assertion of place. While Nat Turner's conception was cosmic, the world he perceived was Southampton, Virginia, not Africa, not Indian Territory, not other foreign dominions. It was his native ground that he had been called to redeem.

All three men were deeply committed Christians. Gabriel's brother, Martin, was an exhorter and, if anything, even more adamantly in favor of the enterprise. Denmark Vesey's connection with the African Church and Nat Turner's persuasion is clear. There was little African mysticism among them, no call for a return to ancient gods and the spiritual fatherland, although it is true that Denmark Vesey used Gullah Jack and other conjurers to encourage those who were attuned to that spirit. Nat Turner, on the other hand, wanted to make it clear that he was no conjurer and had no truck with it.

In the eighteenth century, when blacks struck against the system or tried to break out of it, it was not uncommon that they acted with white allies. Some said, perhaps because they thought little of blacks, that the whites were the leaders when they acted in concert. However, the racial bifurcation had advanced so far by the nineteenth century that whites, no matter how economically depressed, would have no part of revolution, with or without blacks. In this way, too, blacks would be obliged to draw more upon themselves. Because blacks had become by this time a people of the country —alienated but not alien—and because there was no exit, those who could no longer tolerate the inequality and would transform the system of almost unbounded power by direct and violent action were limited to the modes of these three men. As life for blacks became more closed, the style of Nat Turner became more compelling. That is why Nat Turner, more than others, has come to symbolize defiance under slavery in the United States.

By the mid-nineteenth century, the only practical way out of slavery was escape. Yet, to escape from the Deep South was almost impossible. The distances were long, the countryside hostile. The average slave traveled little and knew very little beyond his neighborhood. Pursued by patrols and dogs, slaves were not likely to get far; and even if they managed to escape the vicinity, they probably would be stopped somewhere along the way. Lacking a forged pass or papers, or having them but looking suspicious, they would be taken up again and eventually returned to their masters, facing punishment and likely sale to another place.

Most fugitives in the Deep South escaped only for short distances from their places and for short periods of time. They might have been provoked by some specific act—a beating or a job demotion; they would hide in the country, often visiting the plantation or neighboring ones, where they would be given food by other slaves. Sometimes, fugitives were merely trying to get back to a place where they had previously lived, to find a wife or children left behind. Those who were persistent in their efforts to rejoin their families were on rare occasions successful in persuading the white men involved to make the necessary sales. More often, they were sent farther away from their loved ones.

It was much less difficult to make it to freedom from the Upper South. Not only was it easier to reach cities like Philadelphia and New York from Maryland and Virginia, or to gain freedom across the river from Kentucky or Missouri, but the fugitive was more likely to find help among free blacks and some few whites. With more free blacks around, a refugee had greater chance of getting by with forged papers than he had in the Deep South, where he would be an oddity even if legitimate. With care, one could get help in the way of food and information from local slaves. The metaphorical underground railroad was made up of such men and women, slave and free, who sped a swelling exodus on their way to the North. After 1850, the refugee was in constant jeopardy. There were always those, anxious for a bounty, who would apprehend blacks on the streets of Philadelphia, New York, and Boston, bringing them to trial as fugitives to be returned to slavery. Free blacks had to be especially careful in river cities like Cincinnati and towns close to the Southern borders. Kidnappers, under the guise of arresting fugitive slaves might take anyone who could not prove his liberty. The net ensnared indiscriminately those who had been slaves as well as those who were actually free but could not prove it. The federal law, if nothing else, made the entire country a slave society. If the refugee could make it to Canada, he would be safer, but even there he could not be sure.

The decision to escape filled one with anxiety and doubt. The fear and concern over the difficulties, the likely consequences of failure, were part of it to be sure, but there was more. The family and ties that one had to a place were a heavy restraint. To leave meant to abandon parents, friends, or children. The desire had to be quite strong to prevail over the knowledge that one would not see loved ones or friends again. The provocation often was, in fact, the sale or the threatened sale of some family member. Ironically, the more stable and ordered the social life of slaves became, the more difficult it would be to break free. The family and the slave community itself were conservative forces in this respect, making slaves bear the ills of the system rather than rupture the web that gave them place and identity. Outside the plantation, on the long road under the North Star, was a dark emptiness, a loneliness that few slaves would want to endure. Even freedom itself, or liberty, lacking the community context in which one had grown, would be a mixed blessing. Of course, it was easiest for the isolated man to work through the thicket of doubt, harder for the mother or father, son or daughter. And it was easier for the urban slave, not merely because cities offered more ready access to freedom but because the rural slave was apt to find his identity in the land and the community of his fellows. Escape was the act of an individualist, and city life created that kind of personality more readily than the plantation. Many thousands fled, but with each it was more wrenching than we have wanted to think.

Most slaves would not become refugees, nor Gabriel Prossers, Denmark Veseys, Nat Turners. They would define their problem differently. As life for them stabilized somewhat, most would have a stake in order; that is, they would endeavor to hold the family and the group together. To find room in which to live as human beings and to find ways to improve life became primary goals for by far the greatest number of slaves. Threats to order, even from black insurrectionists, were threats to the marginal existence that slaves had carved out for themselves and would strive to protect.

They could be inspired by individual acts of defiance, remembering to the end of their lives the personal courage of the slave who had refused to be whipped, challenging death and on occasion winning. But they could be ambivalent about uprisings that meant disruption all around them. This attitude explains why Nat Turner's army encountered resistance from some slaves. It was not so much that they were loyal to their masters or the slave system; rather, they were loyal to their homes and their order. If Nat Turner had killed their masters and destroyed their places, not only would they have remained enslaved, but most likely they would have been disposed of, dispersed across the land.

Slaves had good reason to be anxious about disorder. Convulsions like the Nat Turner rebellion were always followed by widespread repercussions, including the indiscriminate killing of blacks. Even the whites of Southampton County were shocked at the loss of life and injury to their human property. They were glad to call a halt to the hysteria with the hanging of Nat Turner. The publication of his "Confessions," which proclaimed him to have been the sole leader, ended the episode. Certainly, many blacks in Southampton and abroad would have reason for deep personal regret that Nat Turner was driven by his vision. However spectacular the heroism of slaves like Nat Turner was, most slaves saw the survival of themselves and their families as depending on restraint from acts of desperation.

The stoical ethic of the slave who withstood the system was consistent with certain African and Christian values. Some called slaves fatalists because they seemed resigned to their condition. But their fatalism has to be qualified. They accepted, through their faith, their own worthiness as children of God. They had no doubt that they, in their essence, were as capable of freedom as anyone; indeed, they assumed freedom to be their right. It was neither their character nor divine will that had made them slaves. Their condition was circumstantial. Their struggle against their condition, no matter how righteous a fight it was, would be futile as long as circumstances remained unchanged. They were fatalists in that they would accept their condition and make the best of it. But they insisted that their condition was not inevitable in the mind and spirit of God. Their Bible was filled with examples of deliverance. In time, the circumstances would change and they would assume their rightful place. Thus, slavery was their condition, not their destiny. While their fatalism might see a person as a mule tied behind a wagon, which he must follow willingly or reluctantly, it was nonetheless important for the soul to sound an everlasting, personal nay even as he followed.

White contemporaries and some historians have taken this prevailing attitude as a suggestion that slaves were content with their lot. Far from it. They tried to find a modicum of happiness within brutalizing circumstances. To withstand what would be the negation of their humanity, yet with dignity and honor in the eyes of God, constituted a virtue in their eyes. There is a heroism in this, but we must consider their ethical framework to appreciate it.

Slaves understood and accepted, as few of their masters could, that pain was as much a part of life as pleasure. From infancy, the slave's experience was so filled with pain, the anticipation of pain, the witnessing of pain in others, that there could be no surprise or shock when the lash stung against one's back or when one's heart was crushed in the sorrow of separation. White Americans had always thought of the pursuit of happiness as a right. The weight of pain was not their inheritance; rather, it was something that could be minimized or avoided.

In learning to accept pain and injury as natural to the human condition, the slave came to see the Socratic truth: the true damage to the soul was not in injury inflicted by others but in inflicting injury on others. The righteous person could not be forced to act unjustly, so it was he alone who could inflict injury on himself. The soul of the righteous person was untouched by the pain of the whip unless the person succumbed to self-debasement, fear, anger, or depressing grief because of it. In such a view, the righteous person would remain virtuous even under a tyrant.

The ideal person was one who had sufficiently pulled himself outside the circumstances of his life so that the quick of his emotions remained inviolate to the vagaries of life. Women had often to sustain months of pregnancy and the trial of labor only to give forth a stillborn child; or even more painful, they had to watch many of their children die in their early childhood, yet hold themselves against despair. After nurturing for years the hopes for freedom, slaves often watched them thwarted by the sudden death of a master—a forgotten or ignored promise. Slaves also were often to experience the rending of life from beloved life on the auction block—reason, prayers, and pleadings availed naught. And there was, as there is in all tyranny, the shock of sudden violence that would blow away someone loved, respected, or dear. Against these hardships, the lash was perhaps the least of them, but it too cut deep with pain for those who bore it and for those who looked on in helplessness, bathing the wounds in the private corners of their nights.

To survive whole, slaves had to bear this pain, these injuries, these insults to their humanity, and move on with their daily routines. Some whites came to feel that slaves were unfeeling about family losses. That was a curious and self-serving distortion. Slaves' wounds and hurts were deeply felt, and they showed it; but they knew very well that whatever the loss, life abides, and they must pull themselves through their hurt. Time, like flowing waters, would spill over the emptiness of personal losses, would wash away surface pain. Ideally, they would find an emotional self-sufficiency that protected against shattering events, an irreducible center that would hold fast whatever the shocks outside. Yes, it meant the ability to hold oneself together after one's wife or husband or children were taken away, or after one's hopes had been dashed by the failure of a master's estate, his duplicity, or his death. To the stoic, undeserved suffering is redemptive, and the slaves had a model ever before them:

> They nailed him to de cross
> An' He didn't say a mumbelin' word.

The central ethical demand for the slave was duty, to accept one's duty and to be honest in it. Most saw themselves obliged by their condition to labor for their owner on his place. This was no comment on the rightness or justice of slavery. It was merely to say that given their predicament, there was an honorable way of surviving it, and it was their duty to find that way and live it. This was different from St. Paul's admonition: "Slaves, obey your masters." The duty the slaves honored was inward and, if anything, a respect for their heavenly master.

It is always surprising to find among the many letters from blacks who managed to escape notes of apology to their former owners. They would say they were sorry they had had to run away, and they often offered to compensate their masters with money. Surprising, but it was a frequent occurrence, and it gives us an insight into an ethical makeup that conceived duty as the principal imperative. Sometimes those letters betrayed what the writers felt: a self-conscious moral superiority to their masters.

It was this sense of duty, for instance, that drove Solomon Northup, a New York free black man who had been kidnapped and enslaved in Louisiana for twelve years, to persist in the precious secret of his free condition until he found the right messenger to get word to his friends in the North. How else to explain Josiah Henson's loyalty to his master, who, apparently in debt, had asked Henson to "run away" with eighteen of his slaves, taking them to a brother in Kentucky? Henson did that, resisting the temptation to escape when he had his charges in Cincinnati. He had given his word to his master that he would be responsible for their safe conduct from Maryland to Kentucky, and he was a man of honor. He was neither a stupid man, nor was he servile. He simply felt himself bound by duty and the obligation of living up to responsibility. In time, Henson did escape to the North and to Canada, but he did that after discovering his master's duplicity: the white man had taken Henson's money in the way of payment for his freedom, but his plan was really to sell him into slavery in the Deep South. Absolved of any sense of duty, Josiah Henson felt justified in fleeing.

Slaves had sufficient reason to strike out at the institution, escape, or engage in any of numerous acts of individual resistance. We need not search for motivation. However, it is remarkable to note that most slaves who left a record of why they refused any longer to serve mentioned some felt betrayal of them by their masters. For those who were bound by duty, such an action was often necessary to make an act of defiance honorable in their eyes. Contrary to St. Paul, their duty was not to their master; their duty was to do right.

A stoical ethic was appropriate to a people whose lives were defined in terms of limits, restraints, and pain. It was quite contrary to what the mainstream of America had come to accept, for in the burgeoning, expanding, continent-conquering pre-Civil War decades, most Americans could imagine nothing to limit their possibilities. It was an optimistic world except for some who would be haunted by a Calvinistic insight into the corruption of the human heart. They would remember that limits were to be honored, that human arrogance was often hubris, and that the true Christian must have a contrite heart. They would find in the famous novel of Harriet Beecher Stowe a great and moving beauty, not because it described or attacked slavery but because it honored a true heroism in an orthodox Protestant view. One aspect of whites' complicated and contradictory view of blacks and slaves was their belief that blacks had a greater capacity for genuine religious feeling, that they were more truly Christian, than whites. It was the slaves' stoical quality that they detected.

Slaves accepted the pain inflicted by whites and blacks with a remarkable capacity for forgiveness. It is the genius of stoicism that the victim, the oppressed, can convert pain by transcending it, gaining a moral superiority over the oppressor.

The slaves' tendency to adapt to their condition rather than to defy it attests to their realism rather than their contentment or inertia. Never did Afro-American slaves assent to the rightness or condition of slavery. What prevented their liberty were circumstances, not character. Thus, when the circumstances began to change, slaves were ready to assert what they had always felt: that their rightful place was as a free people.

When the Union Army entered slave country, it sparked a movement of black people that could not be controlled. At the slightest rumor of Yankees in the neighborhood, swarms of men, women, and children sought what they hoped would be sanctuary within the Union lines. They left their masters, often taking guns and horses with them. They asserted their freedom by voting with their feet. These flights from enslavement, across country infested with Confederate soldiers and patrols, incurred great risks and danger. Hardly was this proof that they were fatalists who had come to accept their lot.

Typically, the Union government and its army officers failed to appreciate the heroism of these escapees. They called the people "contraband," the confiscated property of the enemy. Similarly, in three years of war, President Lincoln and his government ignored—as the nation always had—the contradiction of a free society resting on property in human beings. The federal government would have been content for the South to end its secession and keep its slaves; it wanted a war of limited liability: the Union preserved and slavery maintained, if that were possible. But the war wore on at great cost, while Northern and Southern blacks, by the weight of their presence and persistence, forced the issue. They, with the war behind them, made slavery rather than nationalism the principle issue. Male slave refugees transformed themselves from "contraband" into an army for their own liberation.

The black men's fight for freedom, even after it became official, had always to contend with the deep-seated hostility of white officers and fellow soldiers. Black soldiers received lower salaries than whites, were subjected to humiliating discrimination by their own army and brutal atrocities by the enemy, and were grudgingly honored for their valor. They were forced to stand by, helpless, while their wives and children were sent from army camps back into the hands of former masters—either that or left to die from starvation or exposure. It took a powerful will to be free to overlook the infirmities of the Union Army as an instrument of liberation.

For Southern blacks who remained on plantations, it was not an easy thing to accept the "liberating army." The Union Army were not gentlemen. They often were little different from the rabble who made up the slave patrols. Blacks bore the brunt of their scourge. The fields that were ravaged, the precious food expropriated, reduced their already meager diet. They had known hunger before, but to know the hell of war was to endure the sharp bite of starvation. Black women were far more likely to be the victims of rape than their white mistresses, who complained of rudeness and rough treatment at the hands of Yankee soldiers. Yet there were some white soldiers and officers who felt themselves saviors and missionaries, and black soldiers (some of them former slaves) who talked of liberty and freedom, and lifted up their hearts.

The disorder and ruin brought by contending armies might appear as the dawn of a new day or, more likely, as unmitigated chaos. One could not know the shape things would take from moment to moment, so the deeply instinctive peasant conservatism of the slaves led many to hold themselves quiet and to focus on what was familiar until things were settled. Many pulled close around those they knew and could trust, and tried to hold things intact. They protected their kin as best they could and tried to find security in their white familiars. They might protect the mistress and hide away what was left of the family's wealth. In years to come, sentimental white folks would cherish such memories as justification of themselves and of the old order.

Slaveholders had always interpreted slaves' motivation in self-serving ways. The war experience was no exception. Part of their confusion was that they had always believed their slaves' loyalty belonged to them. When slaves showed them affection, it was seldom seen as a free gift of love but as something due them for being good masters. Thus, it was natural for them to see such evidence of loyalty as something they deserved. What they failed to perceive was that the slaves' loyalty to order and to the physical place that was their home was a different matter.

With the war's end, freedom came as a legal fact. In principle, freedmen were their own persons, owned by nobody, free to move. And they did move about the country, but most of their travels were in search of wives or husbands, children, and kinfolk. It was an effort to pull together the raveled ends of their lives and reweave a whole fabric. It was a search for order rather than anarchy. Even those who stayed put often did so in the hope that dispersed kin would know where they could be found.

If they could have had it their way, they would first have ordered their family lives: made their marriages legal and secure, gathered their children to them, made contact with all who could be recalled. Then they would have found a way to make their labor support their families; they would have educated themselves and their children. What they did and said in the first years of freedom tells us that. But they were not to have their way.

Many white Americans like Abraham Lincoln himself, wished a means could be found to transport all Afro-Americans to Africa. They sensed, quite correctly, it was not slavery that had made the nation a "house divided"; it was race. The fissures cut deep to the foundation. But blacks could not be wished away any more than the nation could have been wished into being without them. The South was what its land produced, and the land would yield what black hands could coax from it. Thoughtful men, black and white, knew that would be so far into the future.

No longer slaves, black people expected to continue on the land. There was no meaning without place. But they expected their relationship to the land to change. Before the war, both they and the land had been the property of others. Now, they were no longer property and the land could be theirs.

However, whites wanted it otherwise and had the power to impose their will. Blacks were no longer their property, but neither would they be independent as long as they were landless. The war and emancipation had expropriated slave owners' human property. Billions of dollars of marketable value had been wiped away with the Thirteenth Amendment, but those who would be able to hold the land still would control the future.

For the slaves, there had been an expropriation of an even greater magnitude. For nearly 250 years slaves had enriched the South and the nation with their labor, but their compensation over the generations had been mere subsistence. Free labor would, of course, have accumulated to itself some share of the economic growth it had created, but slaves had nothing. Ironically, emancipation brought this fact down with telling force. The lives and struggles of their forebears added up to naught. The newly freed slaves owned themselves, and that was all. They were denied any claim to the land they and their forebears had worked or against owners whom they had enriched. They stood on the threshold of their new day with nothing but their hands, hopes, and dreams.

Thus, the opportunity that follows in the wake of wars—falling land prices, the chance for quick and easy fortunes from speculation and rebuilding—would benefit only whites of the North and South who had the capital and cunning to take advantage of the situation. Black men and women would become pawns in such men's calculations, essential as the land was essential, but as powerless to change things as the land itself.

The war left untouched the assumptions and myriad conventions defining blacks out of the community, denying them a free, competitive role in the pursuit of their happiness. Race relations in the South (and in the rest of the country, for that matter) remained an issue of force, the dominion of power rather than law. And blacks as a powerless people had to recall techniques learned in slavery to deal with tyranny.

Free blacks in the antebellum South had long known that for survival the aegis of a white person of influence and power was a necessity. As the freedmen's political rights eroded during Reconstruction, they would seek to lean on the feeble reeds of the Freedmen's Bureau and the Union Army. But after federal support was withdrawn and blacks faced the lawlessness of white mobs, they had to retreat from assertions of promised rights and seek the protection of white men of property. Those who would be independent needed a day-to-day courage seldom demanded of other Americans, and they often paid with their lives.

In the end, all of the flash and the glory and promise of the new freedom would be denied. The guns, the lash, the fagot, and the hangman's rope would smother freedmen's hopes, all under the nation's indifferent eyes. In their lifetimes, most of the freed men and women would be reduced to a near peonage, denied almost every right of citizenship, whatever the Constitution had been made to say. For too many, what freedom meant in the end was continued oppression and brutality without the meager security plantation life had provided. For all black men and women, regardless of where they finally settled, the realization sank in that America, not only the South but all of America, would remain for them a land of tyranny.

EPILOGUE

Sic Semper Tyrannis

WE ARE DRAWN even now to that Dutch ship that lay off Jamestown in August 1619. We might well wonder about the thoughts and visions of those first twenty Africans who stood there, poised on the edge of history. They foreshadow us all, white and black, into our own time.

The loss of their past was hard upon their spirits. They had come a long way to arrive at those shores. Far in miles, of course, but even further as human experience and imagination are measured. Could they but have willed it, they would undoubtedly have awakened themselves, as from a dream, to be in their own fields or huts, only bewitched. But that once familiar and certain world had become for them a phantom. They felt defiled and abused, and they harbored an anger and rage that would be passed from generation to generation, like an Afro-American gene. Had it been in their power to do so, they would have killed their captors and made off for Africa.

But was there not something else in their minds and hearts as they stood on the edge of this new world? Did not the continent, rising before them strange and unknown, seduce them as it did others who imagined it or

244

saw it for the first time? Did it not excite in them, too, a capacity for wonder? Were they no less newcomers than the white men of Jamestown, whose tenuous hold on the continent forced them to depend upon a people so different from themselves?

Neither those twenty Africans nor John Rolfe, who recorded their arrival, could have known the story that would soon unfold between Africans and Europeans in that new world. But they all must have shared a sense of the enigma of America. Uncertainty, the act of being engaged in an unknown and evolving future, was their common fate. In the indefinite was the excitement of the possible. The Africans had only their bodies and their wits as resources, but those qualities might be enough to help shape a still inchoate future. The mind might mold it into a dream that could be held on to. In that was the soul of the American experience to come. A little over a century later, Thomas Jefferson would articulate it as an inalienable human right: "the pursuit of happiness."

That sense of possibility and that dream have infected all Americans, African no less than European. Perhaps that explains why those few Africans—such as Cinqué and Ayuba Suleiman—known to have escaped from American slavery and returned to Africa were never quite able to resettle into their familiar world.

Yet the dream had been elusive to us all, white and black, from that first landfall. Afro-Americans have so often stood on the threshold, the dream so close we could hardly fail to grasp it, only to have it slip away just as it must have done that August day in Jamestown. The dream would be revealed in the rhetoric of human rights at the nation's founding. When one reached out, the promise of a "new birth of freedom" proved insubstantial. Black men would fancy they could win it with martial and manly courage. And some thought they had captured it with Jackson at New Orleans, Shaw at Fort Wagner, Pershing at San Juan Hill, the French at Meuse-Argonne; but such hopes were in vain.

There would be new beginnings, each reliving some of the wonder and promise of Jamestown. Those valiant folk who took their first perilous, fugitive steps on a path that should have led to freedom in the North; those adventuresome ones who struck out for Kansas and the West to make their way to cattle towns or mining towns or to the Pacific Coast; those enterprising people who had been borne by railroad or subway to their first landfall on Seventh Avenue or South Parkway or the other axes of black urban life—all must have seen that same phantom promise in a future just beyond their grasp.

With each achievement a new corner would seem to have been turned, so one would indulge pride in the first black person to have been admitted, to have been accepted, to have made it somewhere. It would be the same in the celebration of the black presence in art, in music, in business, in politics. Yet each turning seemed to lead back to the same place. The waves against the shores pulled incessantly back to those first beginnings, the first lost chance of America to become.

Occasionally a white man—a Melville, a Whitman, a Twain—would feel the canker on the heart and see that the dream had eluded white folks too. Most white Americans, however, would remain victims of their power to own and possess everything but the essential. Their capacity to wonder twisted into an art of self-deception. So with those Virginia owners of slaves who, fresh from their victory over the British, took as the motto of their new policy (which they called a commonwealth) *sic semper tyrannis*, oblivious to the irony.

There have been those rare moments when white Americans and black Americans have stood together and seemed able to overcome the burden of their mutual history. A rare few have helped us look into our own hearts and see the continent rolling ever westward so that we might behold what those twenty Africans saw in the new land and world they would help to make.

But in those first times, what appear to have been decisions casually made foredoomed disaster. The decisions would be repeated again and again, not just to exploit black people for profit but to despoil other human resources; not just to expropriate the substance of people but to ravage the land and water and air. The high price paid for these sequential disasters rests not only in the trauma exacted on the victims, not only in the outer dimensions of the ruins, but in the collective trauma, the loss of community, that has plagued us as a people. It has meant that when we have most sensed our greatness, we have been made to feel our meanness; when we have proclaimed our freedom most, the ghosts of slaves have sung loudest in our ears; when we would finally grasp the dream, we were stunned by our failure of heart and imagination.

What would appear to be a paradox is at bottom contradiction. The shadows and ghosts of the past remind us that those who would be tyrants cannot be called free men.

> So we beat on, boats against the current,
> borne ceaselessly into the past.

> —F. Scott Fitzgerald
> *The Great Gatsby*

Bibliographical Note

THE BOOK that I have written has not called for foot-notes and such marks of scholarship. I would, however, want the reader to be aware that such books as this cannot be written without considerable research and the work of other scholars. I have rested on others, and it would be well to say a word about them.

Several books will help the general reader who wants to know more about West African history and the slave trade. Basil Davidson's *A History of West Africa to the Nineteenth Century* (1966) is still the most convenient introduction to the literature. Carlo M. Cipolla's *Guns, Sails, and Empires: Technological Innovation and the Early Phases of European Expansion, 1400–1700* (1966) is a fascinating study of the technology that led to the development of the transatlantic slave trade.

Philip D. Curtin brought together some narratives of West Africans in his *Africa Remembered: Narratives by West Africans from the Era of the Slave Trade* (1968). In addition, his *The Atlantic Slave Trade: A*

Census (1969) is a comprehensive inquiry into the actual numbers of persons involved in the trade. There are two very good and very readable books on the slave trade itself. Basil Davidson's *The African Slave Trade: Pre-Colonial History, 1450–1850*, originally published as *Black Mother: The Years of the African Slave Trade* (1961), puts the story against the backdrop of African history. Daniel P. Mannix and Malcolm Cowely's *Black Cargoes: A History of the Atlantic Slave Trade, 1518-1865* (1962) attends to the techniques of the trade. W. E. B. Du Bois's *Suppression of the African Slave Trade to the United States of America, 1638-1870* (1969) remains important even though it was first published in 1896.

Modern scholarship on slavery in the United States begins with Kenneth Stampp's *The Peculiar Institution* (1957). It was Stampp who first made effective use of the insight that Afro-American slaves were human beings and, thus, freed historical discussion from the blatant racism that distorted earlier works. After twenty years, this book is still the place to start.

Since the 1960s, it has become easier for the general reader to read the testimony of slaves on their own experience. There are a number of editions of narratives of ex-slaves who found their way to freedom in the antebellum period. Gilbert Osofsky collected three of them in *Puttin' on Ole Massa* (1969). One can read with profit the ones Osofsky collected or several others.

There was a different kind of narrative about slavery—that collected by interviewers in the 1930s. The most comprehensive of these collections is the multivolume work by George P. Rawick, *The American Slave: A Composite Autobiography* (1970). There are many one-volume collections. Among them are Ben-

jamin A. Botkin's *Lay My Burden Down* (1945) and
Norman R. Yetman's *Voices from Slavery* (1970).

Unquestionably, the most important book to come
out of this interest in slave narratives is Rawick's *From
Sundown to Sunup* (1972) in which the author dem-
onstrates how this material answers questions historians
have always asked about slavery.

The most recent histories of slavery have been enriched by this previously untapped source. Notable are:
John W. Blassingame's *The Slave Community* (1972),
which was the first serious exploration of slave com-
munality; Leslie H. Owens' *This Species of Property*
(1972), which gives a full textured picture of slave
life; and Eugene Genovese's monumental *Roll, Jordan, Roll* (1974), which is especially remarkable for
its sensitive and provocative discussion of slave religion.

There have been some noteworthy books touching
on slavery in colonial America: Gerald Mullin's *Flight
and Rebellion* (1972), Winthrop Jordan's *White Over
Black* (1969), and Edmund S. Morgan's *American
Slavery, American Freedom* (1975).

Three recent books stand apart for breaking really
new ground about the world and mind of the slave.
Peter H. Wood's *Black Majority: Negroes in Colonial
South Carolina from 1670 Through the Stono Rebellion* (1974), unlike other histories, shows the forming
of America to have been due to the mind, imagination,
and craft of Africans as much as Europeans. Herbert
Gutman's *Black Family in Slavery and Freedom*
(1976) establishes a firm and documented basis for
understanding the black family and kinship, and dis-
covers, thereby, a belief-system that was independent
of Euro-Americans. Lawrence W. Levine's *Black Cul-*

ture and Black Consciousness (1977) is the first effort by a historian to explore the Afro-American mind through folk music and folk tales.

There are valuable studies of a more specialized character. Ira Berlin's definitive *Slaves Without Masters: The Free Negro in the Antebellum South* (1974) and Marina Wikramanayake's *A World in Shadows: The Free Black in Antebellum South Carolina* (1973) are both excellent. Arthur Zilversmit's *First Emancipation: The Abolition of Slavery in the North* (1967) is solid and important. Eugene H. Berwanger's *Frontier Against Slavery* (1967), Larry Gara's *Liberty Line: The Legend of the Underground Railroad* (1961), Robert S. Starobin's *Industrial Slavery in the Old South* (1970), and Richard C. Wade's *Slavery in the Cities: The South 1820-1860* (1964) are all essential.

I have found the work of Eileen Southern in *The Music of Black Americans* (1971), Lynne Fauley Emery in *Black Dance in the United States, 1619-1970* (1972), and J. L. Dillard in *Black English* (1972) to have been helpful.

A special word should be said about some of the work of Howard Thurman. His *Deep River: Reflections on the Religious Insight of Certain Negro Spirituals* (1945) and *The Negro Spirituals Speaks of Life and Death* (1947) brought slave religion into serious discussion for the first time, and has often been the starting point for recent historians. His *Jesus and the Disinherited* (1949) gave me particular insight into the religious predicament of the Christian slave.

About the Author

NATHAN IRVIN HUGGINS, Professor of History at Columbia University, prepared for this book through research in Senegal, Ghana, Nigeria, and other African countries, as well as in the major archives of the American South. He has also written *Protestants Against Poverty* (1971) and *Harlem Renaissance* (1971), and edited *Key Issues in the Afro-American Experience* (1971) and *Voices from the Harlem Renaissance* (1976). His articles have appeared in a variety of magazines and journals.

While continuing his teaching at Columbia, he is now beginning work on a forthcoming biography of Frederick Douglass.

About the Author

How Great thou Art.